SHIFTING GEARS

How to Harness Your Drive
to Reach Your Potential
and ACCELERATE Success

RYAN O'REILLY

New York

SHIFTING GEARS
How to Harness Your Drive to Reach Your Potential and ACCELERATE Success

Published in New York, New York, by Morgan James Publishing. Morgan James and The Entrepreneurial Publisher are trademarks of Morgan James, LLC.
www.MorganJamesPublishing.com

The Morgan James Speakers Group can bring authors to your live event. For more information or to book an event visit The Morgan James Speakers Group at www.TheMorganJamesSpeakersGroup.com.

Shelfie

A **free** eBook edition is available
with the purchase of this print book.

CLEARLY PRINT YOUR NAME ABOVE IN UPPER CASE

Instructions to claim your free eBook edition:
1. Download the Shelfie app for Android or iOS
2. Write your name in **UPPER CASE** above
3. Use the Shelfie app to submit a photo
4. Download your eBook to any device

ISBN 978-1-63047-852-0 paperback
ISBN 978-1-63047-853-7 eBook
ISBN 978-1-63047-854-4 hardcover
Library of Congress Control Number:
2015917372

Cover Design by:
Rachel Lopez
www.r2cdesign.com

Interior Design by:
Bonnie Bushman
The Whole Caboodle Graphic Design

In an effort to support local communities and raise awareness and funds, Morgan James Publishing donates a percentage of all book sales for the life of each book to Habitat for Humanity Peninsula and Greater Williamsburg.

Get involved today, visit
www.MorganJamesBuilds.com

Habitat
for Humanity®
Peninsula and
Greater Williamsburg
Building Partner

To my wife, Annemarie:
My true soul mate has been there for me always and has
proved time and time again that she is stronger, kinder, and
funnier and truly fits the description of the "better half."
Thank you.

To Michael, Emma, and Liam:
Chase your dreams with thirsty abandon,
trust yourself—go for it.

Love, Dad.

CONTENTS

INTRODUCTION

"Just do your best!"
—My dad and my hero: **Michael O'Reilly**

Location: Remote Airport. 11:32 p.m.

It was late at night in an empty, cold airport departures area. The lounge would have been luxurious, but I wasn't in there. I was trapped in a desolate, done-for-the-day type of place. Rows of seats along the closed gates sat vacant, waiting patiently for the next day's onslaught of passengers. There were empty seats except for one—mine.

A lone cleaner mopped the long hallway and whistled a low tune. My seat was like all the others: hard-to-get-comfortable, slide-off-the-end types. And for someone who is tall like me, it was extremely difficult to get settled. After an hour of trying to relax, I gave in and let the seat win. I balanced on it half-on, half-off in a long stretched position. I wonder if anyone has ever fallen off these dastardly seats. My laptop bag was at my feet, my travel suitcase to the right.

I looked out the window and saw a dimly lit runway and falling snow. It was the end of my time in Eastern Europe. My wife expected me to be home a full five hours ago. But instead of sitting in front of a hot, home-cooked meal, I choked down a terrible airport sandwich. Inclement weather forced me to change plans and catch a bus from Vienna, Austria to Brno, Czech Republic to this lonely airport. It was the best option and I hoped it would have me home as quickly as possible the next day. Unfortunately, the hotel near the airport was full and a sequence of unfortunate events had me sitting there awaiting the morning's flight.

That night marked the tenth missed dinner with my wife and kids. For anyone who has ever travelled for work, I know you can relate to this scene.

Earlier that day, I had to fire two members of my team: Peter and Ralf. It was day four of firing thirteen people and this was my last country to visit of five.

Five countries—four days. I had insisted on doing the firing face-to-face, even though my boss at the time wanted me to communicate the bad news over the phone. But these were the people I had hired, worked with, laughed with, and I owed it to them. The firings were part of a corporate divisional restructure and were effective immediately. *At least it's done, now*, I thought. I felt tired, cold, and in need of a shower, I sat there absolutely drained and burned out. That had been my life for four years—traveling five or six days a week, six weeks out of every thirteen of a sales quarter.

I can't tell you what I would have given to see my smiling kids and have more time to spend with them. I felt like I didn't really know them anymore. My kids were six, four, and one—too young to understand my sacrifices. Whenever I finally did get home from a trip, usually on a Saturday morning, I was usually too tired or cranky to celebrate and play with them, and it ended in an argument with my wife. Press repeat.

I was burned out, working hard, and not progressing. The wheel seemed to be turning but it wasn't moving me any farther down the road. I began to realize that I was stagnant. My biggest fear was happening—standing still. I realized I had spent the last four years of trying to climb the tricky corporate ladder in an overly political, too-many-chiefs type of organization. It seemed the people who got ahead there weren't the folks who worked hard, but those who told the boss he was always right. Though I was fed up, I still had a small glimmer of hope—hope that if I kept working hard enough, maybe the tide would change.

Sitting there in that cold airport with nothing else to do, I took a long, hard look at myself. I noticed my confidence wasn't anywhere near its previous levels. I began to see signs that I was burned out, stressed out, and in need of change, and not just a small change, either. I had spent the past fifteen years working hard for large high technology multinationals, with eleven of those years in sales leadership roles. Pressure for sales and performance and leadership never once relented over a total of sixty quarters.

How I had loved it in the beginning. Sales had been my passion. It was business mixed with performance, competitive and fast-paced, full of exceptional people (even the ones I didn't like). High-achievers, high-performance companies, and leading-edge technology—what's not to like, right?

The drive for results was constant and unforgiving. "Do more and be more" was always the demand, and I was always happy to comply. It meant achievement, recognition, and commissions in that order for me. It was fifteen years of adrenaline-fueled, hold-onto-your-seats business momentum!

International selling can be like a professional field sports team—win and you are a hero. Lose and you're yesterday's fool.

Those fifteen years had been good to me; I had worked hard, learned to be the leader I always wanted to be, and worked for some of the best leaders out there. I'd love to say I worked directly for Steve Jobs or Tim Cook but I didn't. I was middle management when I worked for Apple. But my leaders and divisional executives were still inspiring and driven. A setback like ill-fated travel would have been a mere blip in my consciousness before now. I would have rolled with the punch like I had for so many years—keep positive, keep going and moving toward the next challenge up the road. I had changed company from Apple to another U.S. Multinational tech company in 2009. This new company had a much different culture to Apple.

But that night in the airport I was despondent and felt myself slipping—from the chair and also away from my personal goals.

That night for the first time in my life, I didn't like where this job was taking me. The emotional strain was now palpable. My back hurt. My energy sucked.

My sleep had been disrupted for months and my mood swings were now more evident and fierce. My marriage was nearly on the rocks. Slouching there in that chair, I knew something had to change. I just didn't know what yet. I felt like work was the biggest burden it had ever been. Work was the largest piece of my misery jigsaw, with all other pieces scattered everywhere.

That was January, 2013.

In the back of my mind, I dreamed of getting promoted, or changing companies. I wanted something—anything—to change my situation. Maybe you've felt the same at some point. Maybe you feel the same right now?

It would take me another nine hours to get the flight home, but another nine months to finally change my situation. I was only nine hours away from a new dawn, but the real dawn was still months away.

I knew sitting there that I had to make a change in direction. Looking back, that moment was the start of an extremely stressful and challenging year.

I saw many examples of lack of accountability, of one rule for one and another rule for the next, of cliques, and "slap ourselves on the back" old-boys' club behavior. Even though I craved interaction and had my faults, this had easily been the worst working environment I had worked in. The gossip and commentary had reached a crescendo of ridiculousness. But it was the pivotal moment of realization—the thinking of "I could do better than this and life should be better than this." I needed to feel the buzz of achievement again and the high of perpetual forward motion.

Even though I was an award-winning leader, I needed to get as far away from the toxic environment where people's self-interest and self-preservation trumped the right thing to do for the business all the time.

Back in 2003, I had been with Apple for seven years. Talk about driven people— and I couldn't speak highly enough of the leadership teams I worked for during that time. They were simply the most driven, dynamic, high achieving people I had ever worked with. It was tough work, but it was the best place I've ever worked. I learned so much from people who worked for me, from my peers, and from the execs and leaders. Those were heady times, but we were never complacent. We were always driving at 100 miles per hour—strap your seat belt on!

Fast forward to 2015, I've left the corporate world and now run my own speaking, executive coaching, and sales training business. I went back to University for the first time in fourteen years and received a professional diploma in business and executive coaching, (and I am currently studying for my Masters degree in Personal and Business Coaching) I learned more about myself in those few months at University and was lucky to share the experience with a great class of future coaches, who I'll be forever grateful and humbled for their support, compassion, care, and help over that roller coaster year. Despite all the setbacks, it was my internal drive that eventually won through. The long hard lessons I learned during that time are shared in the following pages.

I believe in people and their unlimited potential. I believe everyone has success ahead. Not everyone can see it, nor does everyone want it, but for those of you who have dreams and hopes and drive—this book is for you. For you can do anything you want to do, but the first step is the need to recognize the need for change. Observation is what I do best. I recognize and observe people in their environments. I listen to understand motives, baggage, and when I coach I am tapping into the person's potential. I want to believe in them instantly when I meet them. After all, if we have cheerleaders in our lives that believe in us, the road seems less difficult.

I harnessed my own drive to make that change, and today I am my own boss and master of my own destiny. The first thing I wanted to do was to tell people that it happens—change, that is. It happens. We can embrace it, recognize it, drive it, shun it, or ignore it, but like the tide and time—change happens. And it's okay if you feel muddled now about where you are in life. Things will work out—they always do. Brighter horizons wait for you. That's why I called my coaching and consulting company High Potential International, as I believe everyone has it. High Potential. Thanks to the changes I implemented in my own life, I know my kids better than ever and now know their personalities so well. My wife and I have gotten to know each other again and it feels amazing!

That's the reason I wrote this book. If it can help you rediscover your drive to get you going again, then the endeavor has been more than worth it. If it resonates with you and helps you ignite the change you want to see, then that motivates me. I want to see you live up to your full potential. I want that ambition that you know is within you to be unleashed. I want to celebrate your achievements—whether it's running a marathon for the first time, climbing Mount Everest, getting that promotion, completing a goal, or winning that golf tournament—I'm the guy at the finish line cheering you on! The drive guy!

This book is going to help you realize your true potential, and harness your drive to help you reach it. If the lessons here resonate with you, hopefully that will be the catalyst to inspire change.

Of course it's not just people in the corporate world who lose sight of their potential. It happened that way for me and there are millions out there who go through the same phases and emotions. Mothers, fathers, students, sports stars, and celebrities all experience self-doubt and low confidence from time to time. This book is for everyone that has ever experienced what I have just described.

Spinning on the wheel and not moving forward. I hope you enjoy the read.

Just do your best and reach your own potential.

—**Ryan**

CHAPTER 1

DRIVE

I stood with my arms outstretched, my eyes closed. A slight wind wrapped gently on my t-shirt. I was standing on the wrong side of a fence on a bridge. The bridge was named Kawaru, and it spanned a ravine 143 feet above a raging white water river. My breath was fast; I was nervous. *Take it easy,* I told myself. *Chill.*

How did I get here? Am I mad? How has it come to this? I asked myself. I was 13,000 miles from home.

Call it competitiveness, ambition, or whatever describes the trait that drives one to set goals. Call it madness or stupidity. Call it as you see it. I call it *drive.* I've always been driven. If 'they' said I couldn't, then I'd make sure I did.

As a self-conscious, tall teenager, something clicked and I became highly target and goal driven—motivated to do things and get things done. To see and experience things, to avoid mediocrity, to make sure I took my chances and opportunities so that I would never look back in anger. I didn't want to have any regrets from my youth when I was old and graying.

I remember T.S. Eliot's poem the "Lovesong of J. Alfred Prufrock" inspired me one day:

"Have known the evenings, mornings, afternoons,

I have measured out my life with coffee spoons"

I didn't want to end up measuring my life with coffee spoons and from that day forward, I secretly built my dreams and decided to plot my own course without regard for other's opinions or worrying about the people who said "you can't." I always had the opinion that I could, if I really wanted it. I just had to work hard and focus on what I wanted; to stand up and say I would not conform. Everything is achievable with drive.

I started writing lists of what I wanted to achieve, places I wanted to see, people I wanted to meet, career goals, and life goals. You name it and there was a list for it! As you read, I am still writing these lists. There is still plenty more to achieve. I'm not ready for retirement yet.

I spent most of my time as a teenager reading, working, or playing sports. I was good at some sports, awful at others, but I excelled at reading and working. I read everything and anything. I devoured information and insights into my favorite sports personalities, famous politicians, or icons of our age, like Gandhi or Mandela.

Often times I was so moved by these people's struggles and tenacity that I would get moody for weeks thinking of their courage or the obstacles they faced. Frequently, I would find myself comparing my own small issues and coming to the conclusion that to be a high achiever in this life, you had to be willing to aim higher, risk more, and dream big. The most common characteristics from all of these people were: perseverance, courage, and an inherent inner drive for success in their fields of choice.

And funnily enough they ALL set goals and targets for themselves. This was something I started to do and still do to this day.

So back to the bridge. A few nights before, I remembered my "Top 100 things to do before I die" list. I was about to step off this bridge and dive 143 feet into the river below. The bridge was sixteen miles from Queensland in New Zealand, known as the adventure capital of the world. New Zealand had been on my list of places to see and experience, and what better way to start living and finish my Australia/New Zealand travel adventure but to jump off a bridge?

Kawaru Bridge is known as the home of bungee jumping. Bungee jumping (for those of you not in the know) is the art of tying a long elasticated rope to your feet and to jump off a bridge or a ledge with the "rope" being your only "safety net." It is described as an adrenaline-fueled adventure sport. I certainly feel every bit of adrenalin.

I was about to jump and was cursing myself for writing this on my wish list. I like this quote:

"Life is not measured by the number of breaths we take, but by the places, people and moments that take our breath away."

Well this moment was certainly taking my breath away, and I was exhilarated and alive, and looked down into the ravine below.

The attendants started to strap the rope to my feet.

I watched the Scottish guy ahead of me who was about to jump.

"Three…two…one…jump!" the friendly jumpmaster shouted to the guy.

The guy readied himself for the jump, and literally just froze (such is the difficulty of "stepping off" the bridge).

He sat down in protest until they untied him.

I was next.

How was I supposed to follow that?

My father had always told me to give everything 100 percent. "Do your best," he would say. "Don't give up!" Well if he saw me now on this bridge ledge, he'd probably think I was crazy for thinking about it. I shuffled up to the same spot the Scot had just reneged from.

The rope was tied securely around both my ankles.

Looking down, my head got slightly dizzy. It seemed a long way down to the two guys in the rubber dingy who were responsible for un-hooking me when I stopped bouncing around, or for saving me if anything went wrong.

Without delay (and I am sure with an eye on the queue behind me) the bungee attendant said:

"Look out at the trees there—and try and jump as far out as you can. Ready?

Three…two…one…bungee!!"

I jumped and then fell off the bridge.

The adrenaline was pumping. My senses were heightened as the air rushed past. What was in reality ten seconds felt like ten minutes.

Ever have a dream, where you are falling fast and wake up with a jump? That's what it was like! If you've done a bungee jump before, then you know the feeling. If you ever intend to do one, god speed!

I was falling fast. The world seemed to slow down and everything was in glorious Technicolor.

I can actually still remember lots of the details.

All of a sudden the water came to greet me. I prepared myself for hitting the cold river. Luckily, my arms went in elbow deep before the bungee rope kicked in and dragged me back up. Then, it dropped me again and then dragged me back up until finally it stopped. I was upside down, nine inches above the water, swinging at the end of a large elastic band!

As I dangled upside down from a bungee rope 13,000 miles from home, I smiled and thought about where these lists had taken me, how motivated I was by accomplishing them, and how far they had brought me.

The dingy gents got me into the boat and told me my fall was the most ungraceful jump they had ever seen. We laughed a little and then I just continued to smile to myself.

This memory is now I how I open some of my speeches. If it weren't for drive and a determined mind, I would never have traveled so far from home and pushed myself so far outside my comfort zone. Did I mention I had a fear of heights? Not since jumping from a plane on my own when I was eighteen, have I experienced such a thrill.

"The man who can drive himself further once the effort gets painful is the man who will win."

—**Roger Bannister**, the first person to run a sub-four-minute mile.

"That internal kick-starter that keeps you going forwards to the person you want to be despite any or all setbacks."
—Ryan O'Reilly

Driven people become 100 percent focused on where they want to be. They chase that destination and often arrive quicker. Driven people want to become the best in their field. They may be the Rocky Balboas of the world, who have everything to lose, but have everything to gain. Or they may be normal folks like you and me who drive themselves forward or read books like this to help us move faster.

Don't be fooled by drive. It's individual. Everyone has it, but not everyone wants to acknowledge it or use it. Others seem to be super driven toward their own end games. Others still are more altruistic and put the success of the team before themselves. Highly paid team sports have athletes who are driven but who prefer to use that drive to help something bigger than themselves.

Professional athletes are driven. The majority of entrepreneurs and business owners are driven. Extremely successful people aren't the only people with drive though. There are millions who get out of bed every day and work hard and provide. Or like my parents, who drove themselves forward for their family and for survival. Drive is a part of every human being, but what we are driven toward may be different. These days, we admire famous people or celebrities, for their sacrifices or journeys—but driven heroes are everywhere.

Driven heroes are the soldier who wants to walk again after losing his legs; the mom who is determined to get back into the workplace after her kids have grown up; the entrepreneur who wants to be successful and make her idea shine; the college grad who is determined to break into the firm or job that she wants; or the student from an impoverished background who wants to be the first college graduate from his family; or the overweight guy who turns it around mid-life and goes from couch potato to fitness instructor.

We all have that drive—to be better, to strive forward. But with work and pressures to pay the bills and just general life pressures, our goals and dreams get lost somewhere along the way. "Maybe next year," we say to ourselves. There is always a good reason not to drive forward.

That is the challenge.

Driven people believe we can. Look at Angela Ahrendts, Sheryl Sandberg, Sir Richard Branson, Steve Jobs, Warren Buffett, Mark Zuckerberg, and Elon Musk. How driven do you think all of these people were or are? Extremely driven! Remember how powerful that Obama election campaign was? "Yes, we can."

Ever hear of Diana Nyad? Diana swam non-stop 100 miles from Cuba to Florida. She was the first person of any age and gender to make the swim successfully. Here's the interesting part—she failed four times. It was only on her fifth attempt, after repeatedly being stung by jellyfish and vomiting that she made it through. How driven was she toward her goal? In the face of many setbacks, I am sure many told her it couldn't be done. But she did it. She was unbelievably driven and had huge self-belief.

Everyone has potential. Everyone has dreams. The difference is how badly people want it or how clear they are about the path to get there. I've met very driven people who aren't clear on their goals, or feel stuck. I've been there too— where I was adapting too much to the environment I was in and not being true to my self and my own drive.

ARE THERE DIFFERENT KINDS OF DRIVE?

Yes. In my opinion there are. I have a client who is an amateur golfer. We all know one, right? His main drive (excuse the pun!) in life is to become a better golfer. That's what makes him tick the most. He desires or wants to be recognized as a great golfer. Every day he wakes up and focuses on his ambition. He putts before breakfast and uses affirmations like "I am a great golfer" or "I will be the great golfer I know I can be." He knows he might never hit the high professional ranks, but he also knows that on any given day he could beat those professionals. He believes it. It's what drives him forward. It's his internal kick-starter and one day, I have no doubt he will be the champion he deserves to be. He said to me recently "I am beginning to believe the best club in my locker is me!" As a coach I clapped silently when I heard this. Super!

My best club in my locker is me. Whether you are an experienced golfer, or have never raised a club, this should resonate with you. It should resonate with everyone reading this. We are all our best "clubs."

"The Best Club in My Locker Is Me!"

Tim Gallwey in his excellent and thought provoking series, *The Inner game of Work* reminds us that life is about believing that we are part of that locker of clubs and the "inner" game is the one we have to master to progress.

As for the golfer I am coaching, he keeps going from strength to strength on the golf course. He is actively investing in himself to get better and release that natural competitive drive. I'll be there the day he lifts that cup. It's just a matter of time.

Daniel Pink wrote a fantastic and thought provoking book called *Drive—What Really Motivates Us.* It is a refreshing read and a new take on motivation and how people are motivated. He made some fantastic observations. Autonomy, mastery, and purpose are our biggest motivators. These three drive us on more than money or incentives.

Harnessing Your Drive: To Harness Anything Is Powerful

Think what happens when you harness your work team toward a difficult goal and it's achieved. We've all seen what a team of horses can do when harnessed together—good image, right? It's where the term "horsepower" comes from. They become one and are focused as one toward their destination. Or you muster and focus your drive on saving for that foreign vacation. Feels good, right? Or you achieve what others simply said could not be done. What makes us want to gather all our drive toward that goal?

Harnessing your drive can help you accelerate faster toward your goal or destination. Often, successful people are so maniacal about the one thing they are chasing that it becomes personal and almost maniacal. They look at setbacks as challenges, and competition as a motivator. Do you know anyone like that?

The same goes for professional athletes. They build and harness their drive toward what they want to achieve. Sometimes they consume them so much that it's all they see. Recently I read that the world's top golfer, Rory McIlroy, writes his goals on a small piece of paper every year. He writes maybe seven in total—never more than that. He keeps the goals simple and goes back at the end of the year to the same sheet of paper and ticks off what he achieved. I know professional sports teams go through a "driven" goal setting process every year as a team. You hear sports people often commenting that their professional pursuits can be quite selfish at times due to their focused approach.

Let's stop here and take a minute to figure out what drives you:

1. Reflect

Take a moment in a quiet place to reflect on where you have come from. How fast have the last few years gone? Have you achieved what you set out to do? Start a journal, and write a paragraph, or use bullet points. Try to answer as honestly as possible—it's not like you're sharing with anyone else. This is only for you (although you can feel free to share!).

- My biggest goal two years ago was to _____
- I achieved this goal in the time frame expected. **Yes No**
- I felt I gave everything to the achievement of this goal. **Yes No**
- I can say, in hindsight, that I really wanted this. **True False**
- I laughed in the face of setbacks and didn't get derailed on my journey to achieving my goal. **True False**
- Fear raised its head a few times but I drove on. **True False**

2. Role Model

Who is your role model? Is there someone you know who has the kind of drive you'd like to have? Someone who knows what they want and where they are going in life? Is this your brother, your sister, a family member, a good friend, someone who seems to be very successful in their field? What can you learn from them?

- Sit down with them and ask them what drives them.
- Then, ask them what was their biggest success so far.
- Next, ask them to define what drive is for themselves. Take your journal and write notes.
- If you don't know someone who can teach you about their drive, then start observing a sports star or a celebrity, read their books, and listen to their interviews.

For example, the famous and inspiring astronaut Chris Hadfield, decided at the age of six that he wanted to be an astronaut (the same goal I had when I was six by the way!). The difference is what he did next. As a six-year-old he asked himself these questions daily:

- What would an astronaut do in this situation?
- Would an astronaut eat this for breakfast?
- Would he ride the bus to school or run?

Asking these types of questions about everything that came his way helped him to develop an astronaut's mindset and to become driven about his lifetime goal. Everything about being an astronaut took Chris one step closer to being one, by starting to live or model his life on what they do. Now he is one of the world's most famous astronauts and speaks all over the world about how much it meant to him and how driven he was to become one.

3. What Drives You?

The next thing you have to do is answer the above question, then the following:

- Where do you want to be?
- What is your destination/life goal?
- Why do you want to achieve what you want to achieve?
- Who is it for? (This is always a hard one to answer with drive!) Is it for you? Or is it for someone else? Or is it both?

Finally, in front of a mirror, read out your stated "place"/your destination. Look yourself straight in the eye in the mirror (try it and you will be surprised, just be careful not to do it where you can be disturbed).

- HOW BAD DO I WANT IT?
- Did you do it?
- So again, how bad do you want it?
- If you know what drives you, and where you want to be, how bad do you want it? How important is this to you?
- Rate it on a scale of 1 to 10 (1 being "I'm not that motivated" and 10 being "I really WANT this! No matter how long it takes, or what setbacks occur I'm going to get there!" 10 represents the change that you will become one step at a time!):

1	2	3	4	5	6	7	8	9	10

4. Visualization

This is not a new technique and has been used by sports professionals and sports psychologists all over the world. However, the professional and amateur athletes I coach really seem to enjoy these visualization exercises.

Here's a quick way to harness your drive:

- Sit in a peaceful place where no interruptions can happen.
- Relax, breathe, and settle yourself.
- Now, imagine what it will be like to achieve your goal and the emotions you will feel when you get there. How will sleep feel that night or that sense of achievement? Now imagine yourself doing something different every day to get you there. Imagine the possible setbacks and small wins. Imagine your naysayers or people who say "you can't." This will make you feel more determined, not derailed. You will welcome this, as I know you want this so bad that any detractions or negativity will only feed you to get better and become more driven.

- Close your eyes for a few moments.
- How does it feel having seen it come true?
- Practice visualization every time it gets hard or tough or just make a habit of doing it regularly.

I visualize with my eyes closed on how my speaking engagements will go. I picture how I will sound, how I will connect with my audience. I visualize how it will feel. I visualize how I will harness my nerves—yes, all public speakers have them! The power of visualization never ceases to amaze. Standing on that bridge in New Zealand, I closed my eyes and visualized how I was going to push off or jump from the ledge, and as glamorous as it wasn't, I still got myself to do something as a mark of my intent or my drive. It was outside my comfort and well inside my fear.

Golfers visualize the ball going where they want it to land. (If you're like me, no matter how hard I visualize the ball going where I want—it never does! But you get the point!)

5. Think about Your Goal

Spend five to ten minutes every morning thinking about your goal.

Think about your goal, be it in the car, or at the gym or in the shower. Focus on your goals. Check in with yourself every morning. Write down your goals in a place that you will see regularly—home office, fridge, etc. A person I coached recently wrote her goals, laminated them and stuck it beside the bathroom mirror. While brushing her teeth every morning and every evening, she read her goals as a reminder.

- How driven am I today to get to where I want to go?
- How are my energy levels?
- How bad do I still want this?
- Have my priorities changed, if yes, how bad do I want these new priorities?
- Am I continuing to become a more driven person?

Harnessing your drive in the above list of activities will help you jump from small wins to huge success. Asking yourself how badly you want it will help you keep focused on your priorities. We'll talk later about fear and trusting yourself. But for the moment, just think about this: if you harnessed yourself to become more driven and practiced some of the techniques above, will you be able to describe yourself as more driven or to be able to look back and say you completed what you set out to do? My bet is that you will. And we are only on Chapter One!

"It has to become everything to you if you're going to make it to the top. You have to live it."
> —**Monica Seles**, champion tennis player

What made me dive from a bridge so far away from home?

I was driven for the sense of adventure as earlier described. It was thousands of small steps that finally came together in this wonderful moment in this awe-inspiring place. My biggest success wasn't the jump (even though it did give me a sense of achievement); it was challenging myself to go live and work abroad and to get out of my comfort zone. The biggest achievement was the list I had written as a teenager under the section "get out and see the world.".

As you read this book, I've just completed an endurance cycle from the very top of Scotland to the very lowest point in England. John O'Groats (the most northerly point) to Land's End (the most southwesterly point). Yes, the length of the United Kingdom is over 1,000 miles or 1,400 kilometers. I was solo on my bike with just some travel panniers. I am definitely not the first—a plethora of adventure cyclists complete this every year. What made me take on such a task on my own? This is my new way to achieve—test my drive beyond what is normal and see what I can get done. I also used it to raise vital funds for three very worthwhile charities. Being driven for yourself does not mean others can't benefit. I'm using my drive to get myself moving forward and to experience more of this wonderful planet.

THE EDUCATIONAL LEADER, DR. PHILLIP MATHEWS

Dr. Phillip Matthews is currently the president of the National College of Ireland. He was also a former captain of the Irish rugby international team and played for the Barbarians. He was also selected for the British and Irish Lions. For those of you who are unfamiliar with the game rugby is a team sport,—think American football without the helmets and pads.

Phillip is an experienced strategic leader, executive board member, and an active speaker and consultant in executive leadership, 1:1 business/executive coaching, team coaching, and change.

I asked Phillip to define drive for me and here is part of his intriguing response:

> I suppose drive for me is like an unremitting focus. Something within an individual that causes them to pursue something and not be deflected from it. Because in life I suppose there are many setbacks and many other people that will doubt and say it's not valid to aspire to that or you'll never do it. Drive for me just brushes that aside.
>
> I think drive is a—I don't think it's just a personal characteristic— but I think it's a personal characteristic in pursuit of something that the individual is very passionate about. In other words, I might have particular drive in one particular area and therefore be very driven according to some people, but for something else I might not have that same drive. I think what's required is an unwavering belief and a focus and a direction and probably a vision of where that is and a belief that you can get there.
>
> Because I think you need to be resilient against other people who will often introduce their own stuff in terms of your own ambitions.
>
> "Oh, I'm not thinking like that. It's kind of quite threatening to hear somebody else thinking like that so I better pour cold water on it, you know?" Et cetera. That for me is drive.

How do you define drive?

I saw the bridge jump as a badge of my drive. It was uncomfortable and tense, but a reflection of how much I was willing to go through to achieve and be successful. It was also a thrill! It represented how bad I wanted to be different and how bad I wanted to *live*. I suppose I trusted myself a little.

I certainly trusted the rope and the excellent staff. And that brings me to what we are going to discuss next: trust.

In the next chapter we are going to discuss trust and its relationship to drive. Trust me, you're going to enjoy this!

CHAPTER 2

TRUST

The nine months after the overnight in the remote airport were tumultuous. At work, I had given away all of my power to my boss. I battled constantly for validation and became the victim of my circumstances. I hated being the victim. I was angry at how I was being treated. I was angry that my career wasn't jumping to the next level, even though I continued to drive for results and accelerated performance. All I ever wanted was progression. Or, so I thought at the time.

I felt let down and betrayed by some, and wondered what could go wrong next. All of this turmoil had built up over months, even a year or two, and I kept thinking the situation would get better. It never did. I needed a change. I needed to get away from this toxic, cliquish environment and make a clean break.

At home, my wife was losing her patience with me. We argued a lot. It seemed that no one was on my side, and I was battling everyone. I felt my integrity was being questioned. I worried about everyone's perception of me, real or not, and constantly worried about and rethought everything that was said. I'd trust people and get burned. I trusted too many times when it wasn't reciprocated. I was losing sleep and worn out. It was the worst period of time in my life.

Does any of this sound familiar to you?

Every year for the past fifteen, I felt a little more of me slip away. I wasn't ready to be committed to an institution, but I was weary of the odd, egotistic senior leader, and also the politics that can embroil the working day in a multinational environment. One-upmanship and self-interest agendas ruled the roost, at the sacrifice of real relationships and driving the business forward.

People described me as a maverick a few times, and I felt the term was endearing (that was my entrepreneurial side showing). However, I soon realized that being a maverick was my Achilles heel. I was too vocal when I thought execution could be better. My boss wanted someone who would comply, rather than challenge. I was trying to lead in the absence of any real leadership—always justifying my actions to myself on a fairness scale. "This isn't fair!" Or, was this fair?

I was bullied severely at the time, and I'll never forget how that felt. It was awful. My moods were up and down, and I had low energy. But, I still thought if I worked harder, I could make it better. So I did. I worked at showing up brilliantly. And I'd manage to pull it off for a few weeks until the next setback.

The time had arrived to start getting back to myself.

It was time to trust myself and back my dreams once more. That required a giant leap of faith. If no one else would back me, I would have to seek internal validation and back myself.

I am a runner. There's nothing special or extraordinary about my running. I've done a few marathons, but it's what running does for me emotionally and spiritually that's important. Since all of this emotional upheaval started at work, I lost my desire to run. I didn't realize how helpful it had been to my well-being. I was too distracted by everything going on and not focused on me anymore.

Then one winter's day, I ran along the stormy coast, against the wind and rain for hours. I think I ran a total of five hours that day. I tried to run my issues out of me and it definitely helped. That was just the start.

I started to review everything in my life. My most important relationships were, without question and without a second's deliberation, my wife and my kids. I had worked hard for them. It was all for them. My mother, my sisters, and my real friends followed closely in second place. I feared losing everything. I feared living in an apartment on my own, miserable, friendless and maybe seeing my kids on the weekend.

I decided that it wasn't going to go that way. They were far too important to me. I wanted to be there for them, like my mum and dad were there for me—no matter what. I wanted my wife to love me again and feel supported in her role as a stay-at-home mother. I didn't want to be this successful corporate type that was an absentee in everything but paying the bills. I wanted to be present and not miss any more ballet recitals for my daughter, or parent-teacher meetings, or small things at home like birthdays or pizza and movie nights.

One day toward the end of my multinational career, I was in a meeting room with my management team. These people were supposed to be peers and leaders, and some of them I looked up to and trusted. We had to move to a different meeting room. I went to the elevator, and was the first one inside and so I held the door for the others. They all arrived at the elevator, but no one got in. They actually turned around and walked to the stairs together. That's how much of a pariah I had become in the office. It was childish, cliquish behavior from men and women in their forties. It was the final straw. That moment in the lift really upset me. I couldn't be as bad as everyone thought I was. Was I?

It was time for some action.

After the lift incident, I knew it was only a matter of time before I decided to quit. But I wanted to leave on my terms, not theirs. And I did. Walking from the empty lift to the meeting room, I decided I was always going to trust myself first from that point on. No one else needed to validate me anymore. My gut feeling, my ability to get things done, and my drive were going to be my compasses in the future, nothing, and no one else.

I decided my power was mine. *Trust in me*, I told myself.

Leaving a great salary, and a great industry behind in order to chase my dreams was both the scariest and most daring thing I've ever done. It was a huge leap of faith. With my confidence at an all time low, and my self-worth even lower, it was time to make a brave decision. It was my drive and the ability to trust myself that would lead me to be better. Everything that was not adding to this had to go.

I toyed with the idea of charging ahead on my own, but was also open to getting work with a large company again. It was a huge dilemma. Like the old Clash song—"should I stay (with corporate life—just a different company) or should I go (something different, more rewarding, more me) now?"

It was the hardest period of personal change I had ever experienced and one where my personal goals seemed to be floating farther away from me. Emotionally, I was wasted. Something needed to happen to reset my drive and refocus me on the next chapter of my life.

Eventually, it all came to a head. I woke up one September morning, and I had quit the company. I had resolved the situation on my terms. My head felt lighter and clearer. A huge weight was lifted from my shoulders. I was free from the shackles of my previous boss. Finally, I could focus on getting my confidence back.

Over breakfast, I asked myself, *What's next?*

It would have been easy to go through the interview process with other companies, and I am sure I would have found something. But, I could see the scenario turning into the same problem, just a different company. I'd burn out again. How bad would it be the second time?

Coincidentally, a recruiter friend called me right away with an opportunity. The job sounded right down my alley, too. I was excited to be in demand so soon. Maybe this time it would be different.

I sat my wife down and told her the news. Then I saw her facial reaction, and I knew what I needed to do. I dialed the recruiter and said, "Many thanks for bringing this huge opportunity to my attention, it sounds perfect for me. But I have decided to start my own business. I want to empower people. I want to coach. I want to motivate people through speaking engagements, and I want to write—so I won't be going for the interview."

As I waited for her reply, I breathed a huge sigh of relief. I had trusted myself. My life's ambition since I was a kid was to get up and motivate people to teach, inform, inspire, and engage. That's what I received from sales management and leadership. That's all I wanted. It felt good to be true to myself—finally.

Trust is such a big word these days isn't it?

From corporate CEOs, management gurus, every human resources department in the world, industries, insurance companies, you name it, *trust* has become a must have. For those enterprises or people that celebrate dizzying heights of success, trust seems to occur naturally. When it's a half-baked attempt, it seems insincere and fake.

The word "trust" is bandied around too much, in my opinion. When I see "Trust us…" written on a companies literature or website it makes my senses more attuned to how much I should *not* trust them. When a human resources professional tells me to trust them when there is evidence not to, it makes me more aware of that trust element. I still trust people. I believe people need to be trusted, but I am more aware of whom to trust.

As a professional executive coach and motivational speaker, I have to trust myself. Sometimes that means positively holding a mirror to an executive, listening to her, and using myself to help her be more aware of her impact on others. Sometimes it means expertly sensing an audience's participation levels and listening. I have to trust my intuition.

There's no other option, in order for me to grow my business and become the motivator I want to be, I have to trust in my goals and my ability.

"As soon as you trust yourself, you will know how to live."
—Johann Wolfgang Von Goethe

"It takes years to build, thirty seconds to lose, but once you have trust and are known to be trustworthy- people will rely on you because they see you rely on yourself."
—Ryan O'Reilly

One year later and plenty of self-development work later, I went to dinner with my good friend Myles. Myles is a fellow coach and told me, "Trust in yourself."

He repeated it a few times, and added, "Everything will work out, trust yourself."

Trust in yourself.

Great and simple advice, isn't it? Thanks, Myles.

But do we really trust ourselves in our daily lives and decisions? Or are our comfort zones really too comfortable?

The definition of "trust" is where I started writing this book.

"Confident expectation of something; hope," or "to rely upon or place confidence in someone or something (usually followed by *in* or *to*)."

Every day can help you get closer to the person you want to be. The first step is to trust your own self.

I always enjoyed writing, and I wondered if I could ever write a book. The answer came through trust. I trusted myself to be persistent in getting help with writing. I trusted my tenacity when deadlines loomed. I trusted myself that no matter what anyone said or did, that I'd cross the finish line with a completed manuscript that would inspire others to trust themselves.

Trust your drive.

I trusted that my goal of writing a book would realize itself through hard work, determination, and a never-make-excuses-attitude. I was going to drive forward and complete this project, whether I sold one copy or one million. It didn't matter. I just wanted to write a book I was proud of. And after months of writing and editing, I *can* say I am proud of my book.

I trusted myself to tell the truth in this book. Laid bare, honest, emotional—I trusted that it would resonate with someone—maybe you, maybe someone you know. The old me would have said I wasn't good enough, What would others think? Would I meet their expectations? The new me decided the book was for my own self-validation. It was important that my family be proud of the book, too. No one else's opinion mattered.

I trusted that if I wrote honestly about my life experiences and helped someone discover, chase, and realize their full potential, that the exercise would have been worthwhile. That's what drove me.

Recently, I interviewed Jack Black, CEO and course director at Mindstore. Over the last twenty-five years, Jack has spoken to and inspired over a half a million people worldwide at conferences and companies. I asked him, "How should people get unstuck when they're not moving forward?"

He said, "If you were in a field in a car and your car got stuck, you'd do something. You'd get out and try to get yourself out of the 'mud.' In real life, if you were stuck, you'd have to do something different. So many people are stuck in relationships, jobs, or a location, and they don't seem to get that they have to *change* something. In the field, in your car, you would start with the easier things first, you'd physically do something – you'd get out and walk around. The resource to change is inside. When you get yourself very still and very quiet and you listen to your inner voice—that will give you all the direction you need."

Jack also explained that successful people in business or life know that when they need to shift, they feel it naturally, based on their experiences and attitudes.

It's so true!

Author J.K. Rowling showed a huge amount of drive to write and publish the *Harry Potter* series. Publisher after publisher refused her manuscript. Her mother passed away. She endured a divorce. Poverty banged loudly on her door. Yet, she still trusted herself to drive on. She must have had doubts, but thankfully for readers everywhere, she kept going.

She trusted herself to drive on, even though she didn't have any confirmation that a publisher would ever be interested.

Picture J.K. Rowling in your local cafe. She's writing every day there. No one knows her. Publishers have ignored her. But she's there every day, because she's driven to provide for her child and driven to complete this manuscript. She trusts in her story and that of one young wizard. She trusts in her idea. Fast forward a few months, and she never looked back. Harry Potter, born in those small cafes she frequented, was now a star. J.K. Rowling backed herself when no one else did.

SO HOW CAN WE TRUST OURSELVES?

If we trust ourselves, then others will see that confidence and either dislike it or be attracted to it. It's the attracted people you want in your life. There will always be detractors, or as I call them, sheep. People who follow the cool people—we see them in work and life all the time, right?

Learning to trust yourself is a skill that can be practiced. The more you practice, the better you get. Here are some exercises or daily check-ins:

1. **Intuition.** Tune in with your gut feeling. That old adage "trust your gut" is true. Learn how to go with it. Later, we will talk about risk and some tools you can use to make a good decision. But intuition harnessed and used can help you trust yourself.

2. **Journaling.** The best boss I ever had told me he had a learning journal. I was intrigued. He said every day or every couple of days, he would write down when his intuition had worked, and what he had learned from his interactions with his management or teams. He recorded observations around his priorities and personal goals and how he was developing himself. It was very personal information he shared, but I always appreciated it. Since then, I've always kept a learning journal. I don't write in it every day, but I do pick it up regularly and see what I have learned over a time period. It's taught me to tune into that trust and make good decisions about trusting others, especially when weighing opportunities in business and life. Start a journal. Get your kids to start one, too. They'll thank you.

3. **Connecting trust with your goals and drive.** Write down your goals and understand why you want them. Then consider this: Drive + Goals + Trust in achieving your goals = Trust in yourself.

4. **Checking in with your emotional energy.**
   - Do you check in with your energy levels daily?
   - Do you excuse poor energy—because it's Monday, it's raining, it's only work, it was a long weekend, I don't like work, or other excuses—to have low energy?
   - Every morning, rate your energy levels on a scale of 1–10, 10 being the highest.
   - After a week or two, you'll start to notice you can control your own energy just by noticing it. If you control your own energy, then you're going to trust yourself more when you have setbacks or need to trust yourself in difficult situations.

- How is your attitude today? Are you positive or negative? How can you change your attitude right now? The answers affect your energy.

5. **Who do you need validation from?**
   - Is it your family? Friends? Boss? Team? Who needs to validate you and *why*?
   - Take time to answer this one.
   - Then ask yourself, who it is you are pleasing? Is it you or others?

6. **Decide what you are going to accept and not accept and adhere to your guidelines.**
   - What are your values?
   - What boundaries will you place over your power?
   - If things are great at work are they true to your values?

7. **Practice being an inventor of the life you want rather than someone who has life happened to.**
   - We all know people like this. I was someone who had life happen to him during that nine-month spell at a bad job. Are you someone that invents and owns a life plan or waits to see what's going to happen?
   - Write small goals in your journal—things you *know* you can make happen. Then make them happen. You're training your brain to make life happen on your terms.
   - Write bucket lists that you can start doing in life. Remember life is for living after all.
   - Once you step away from the daily and spend time thinking of the YOU of tomorrow—go chase it!

8. **Face your fears and move on.**
   - The next chapter is all about fear. Facing your fears can help you enjoy life more, and trust yourself along the way. What was the last thing you did that really scared you and how did you use that to accomplish your goals?
   - Later, we'll also talk about moving on in our progression chapter.
   - For now, just write down what you're afraid of. You have to identify your fears before you can begin to face them.

9. **Forgive but don't forget.** Forgive what's happened in the past, those who have aggravated or annoyed you. Forgive them. Let it go, but don't forget. Use the memory as fuel. Let it power you forward. It's like having a chip on your shoulder. A healthy chip to be able to be proud of yourself and quietly whisper, "Look at me now."

10. **Be good to yourself.**
    *   Meditate
    *   Enjoy life
    *   Do things that aren't materialistic and about "things" but about people and experiences
    *   Be present

11. **Be kind.** Be kind to yourself and people important to you.

All of these areas, if given enough space, time, and consideration will help your inner trust grow stronger and firmer. Our mental resilience will grow stronger and we will find it easier to make decisions, particularly when it comes to our goals and wants.

In the next chapter, we are going to talk about fear. Most of my coaching clients, I find, are afraid of something. Some know it and like it, others hate it and avoid it. Some folks I have managed over my career were afraid to take a new job or even look for one. Fear gripped them and held them in the same place—stuck.

Don't be *afraid* to turn the page!

CHAPTER 3

FEAR

was seven. It was my first swim lesson. The group was older and more experienced. The swim instructor had a large class of kids. He decided to have a race the entire width of the pool. He told everyone to swim as fast as they could. He didn't mean the instruction to be taken up by his new recruit—me.

I wanted to win. I got about a meter and found myself below the water, looking at the underwater blue-and-white tiled wall. I swallowed a little water and was confused about what was happening. A huge arm came down into the pool and fished me out. The next thing I remember was riding home in the back of the car. My sisters all sat beside me. Everyone was quiet. My mother cried a few silent tears in the front seat.

For years, this memory would haunt me in nightmares as I realized how serious it had been or nearly was. This was my fear from then on: water, drowning.

Move forward to my early twenties. I was in a luxurious hotel pool in Bali, Indonesia. I still couldn't swim. But I enjoyed the water up to my waist. I was in the middle of the pool and hadn't realized the pool had a slanting floor into a very deep end. I slipped down into the deep end. I couldn't get back up the ramp. There was no one else in the pool. Annemarie, my wife—then girlfriend—dove in and went to save me. I am a big guy, tall, and much heavier than my petite wife. My natural reaction was to get out as quick as possible. I started pulling her down to get back to the surface. It was awful. Lucky for me, she was able to get my feet back up the ramp and got me to the side of the pool. I sat at the side of the pool for a while. This swimming lark was haunting me again. Further trauma.

Two weeks after that incident it happened again! I was at a packed beach in Sydney, Australia during the summertime. Everyone there seemed to be in the water. Australia is world-renowned for its rip tides. I was playing it safe. I went in just past my waist to cool down from the high temperatures. It felt like something grabbing my foot, it was like an invisible hand yanking me off the sea floor. My other foot went next. I started to panic. Annemarie was nearby. She remembered the look of fear in my eyes from the pool in Bali. Next I was being pushed out with this strong rip. It was literally like a football player tackling my mid-section and I was pushed right back. Luckily, the woman I would marry, saved my life again, this time without nearly drowning herself. I had been frozen by panic and fear. I got back to a safe area and left the beach.

It was the morning of my first triathlon.

The pre-race buzz was starting to electrify in the early hours, as the competitors arrived, mingled, checked in, and got their bikes ready for transition. For me, sleep hadn't bothered to visit the night before.

Once I parked the car, I immediately switched my iPod on (anything to get me focused). The music was rock, and high tempo and loud. I was about to enter the ring and face my fear. I was focused and confident.

This was my first real competitive swim. My first fifty-meter swim. My first swim in deep water. Three months of swim training in an eighteen-meter pool with no deep end had boosted this non-swimmer's confidence into actually swimming and doing it well. I was pumped, but well outside "comfortable."

So it was important this fear was surpassed so I could get on with my long awaited triathlon career. My stomach was churning since early the day before, that unsettled feeling when we are about to push ourselves out of our comfort zones. I hate comfort zones. I have no idea where or why this started, but I've always pushed myself, trying to break my limits. I hate failure. But when I fail, it's always spectacular and always burns me for a while.

The fifty-meter pool had daunted me the week before in practice, enough to make me stop half way and panic. I had worked hard all week on being mentally focused on the task at hand. "Rhythm. Focus. You want this," I kept repeating to myself all week, along with reading *Mind Gym* by Gary Mack and David Casstevens.

I felt focused and assured I was here to get a job done. The 700 meter swim wasn't that far for anyone who swam their whole life, and some would probably laugh at the thought of being this intimidated by a "small swim in a pool," but this was the day I was going to put to sleep all those experiences and build the confidence to be a good swimmer. I wanted to be capable of swimming a decent distance. This fear wasn't going to get the better of me. I was stronger than that.

The bike and the run are my strengths. I had no worries about those two events. But the swim—that was another story.

I sat at the side of the pool before my wave started just staring at the water. I could feel the anxiety build and I was actively trying to manage it. This was big for me. "700 meters," I thought. "I've done this in training. Let's do it!"

It was a short swim in a pool. Water could hurt me—it had nearly killed me! I never learned to swim until I was in my thirties.

The swim lane for wave two—the "slow wave"— took place in lane 10. The group seemed like a lively bunch and we discussed who was going to be faster than whom so we could get prioritized. This annoyed me a little as there were obviously some swimmers who were out to go as slow as possible. I was there to get my rhythm and keep going. This was my first mistake. I went off second to last. I dove into shallow end (the first ten meters) and three seconds later, I stood up to put on my goggles. This was my second mistake. I started swimming, knowing the drop to the deep end was coming soon, and so I tried to get into a rhythm. My hand hit a foot. This was my third mistake. I should have overtaken immediately. But, fear gripped and reared its vile head and I stopped, and not being a good water treader, grabbed the lane rope. I set off again, and my hand hit the foot ahead of me once more. This was my fourth mistake. Panic and fear onset, and I cursed myself.

My wife, our kids, my mother-in-law, my good friends and neighbors Aidan, Brian, and Deirdre all stood in the viewer gallery with a full on view of my lane. They all knew what this meant to me.

Every length was repeated the same way; I was too fast for some of the other competitors, but with no confidence in my ability to pass them. It was a nightmare. I used the rope four times to pull myself in the last ten meters of the deep end. The lifeguards, high on their chairs, looked down in pity. The officials checked in at the end of every length with passionate looks on their faces.

Then it happened. I swallowed water in the deep end and immediately grabbed the lane rope. When I got to the end, the official asked me nicely to get out.

"We're concerned for your well being. You're now a safety risk, and we're going to have to get you out of the swim." With concern in his voice.

"But this is my first tri…" I said meekly. I could feel the whole pool looking at me. "I'll need your timing chip," he said. "You can still finish the bike and the run, you'll have no official time, but your swim is over."

It was my first did not finish (DNF)—a morning of firsts.

I was gutted, embarrassed, relieved, disappointed in myself. All of those feelings raced through me and emotion was getting the better of me.

I had faced my biggest fear and lost.

I thanked them. They all handled me really well and compassionately. I ran down the side of the pool, not able to bring myself to look up to my kids cheering me on. I could see my wife was crying a little. If I had looked up I would have cried, too.

I ran from the pool, literally and figuratively speaking. As I ran through to the bike transition, my self-pity was replaced with anger. How could failure and fear have snuck up on me so quickly? How was it that I was the worst swimmer on the day when I knew I could go the distance?

I ran my bike out of transition and up to the mount line, twenty kilometers to go. "Right let's show folks what I can offer this race!" I thought to myself.

I cycled past my kids (aged 7, 6, and 3). They were still oblivious to my pool humiliation. They cheered wildly. They were just proud to see dad on his bike. My wife still had tears in her eyes, but I could feel her pride. She knew how much this meant to me. Aidan, the bike mechanic supreme and fellow adventure racer, standing up the road, knew too. But it didn't stop them roaring my name. The look in their eyes is what killed me. I hammered it on the bike, making it my mission to pass as many people as I could. On the turn at the ten-kilometer mark the only thoughts in my head were, "show them you can nail this." Looking back, "show myself" would have been more appropriate. Counting sixteen cyclists who I overtook on the way back, my confidence grew. But, the swim still stung. The five-kilometer run went well. At the finish, the kids were still hyper excited. There were nods of understanding from my wife, Aidan, mother-in-law, and neighbors.

It's never easy failing at something you've had as a big goal for a long time. I was embarrassed and still am plagued with the fear I experienced that day. One day I'll conquer it. The fear hasn't won yet.

That was supposed to be the day I was to conquer my fear of the water. I didn't succeed. However, after that day, I received huge support from folks who had heard about it or read my blog describing what happened in the pool. The messages of support were fantastic and people could relate to the imagery of fear and what it does to us all. It taught me a valuable lesson.

Everyone has fears.

Everyone can relate to facing them.

When fear mugs you and wins, it's hard to get back on track. But I don't like losing to fear. I'm also afraid of failure. Those messages of support will drive me to conquer this fear and win the battle.

Fear has been trying to stop me all my life with varying degrees of success. Can you relate?

Like most youngsters, I was self-conscious and lacked confidence. I went to a boy's boarding school full of competitive, talented, and overachieving individuals. Some of them inspired me by how easily they confronted their fears. Even at a young age, they set high bars for themselves. It was contagious. For this reason, I've always tried to confront my fears and not let them rule me. It was easier said than done. Sometimes the inner-voice wins, and the self-doubt and anxiety hold you back.

The negative voice in my head said things like:

"Why should I achieve this?"

"I don't deserve this!"

"There are others better than me!"

"I am not good enough!"

"What will people think?"

Sound familiar?

It's hard to step away from our comfort zone and willingly go to the place where we push our own limits. The more we push ourselves away from where we are comfortable, the more we need to get a grip on our fear. When we do that, we can actually use fear to help us reach our goals faster.

The youngest ever man to climb Mount Everest was celebrity, writer, and adventurer Bear Grylls. He said about comfort zones:

"The thing about a comfort zone, is that it sounds, well, too comfortable. I call it a comfort pit, because a pit is somewhere you want to get out of as fast as possible."

FAMILY MAN, IRON-MAN, ENDURANCE ATHLETE, AND SENIOR HUMAN RESOURCES EXECUTIVE STEFAN TRAPPITSCH

Stefan Trappitsch has completed no fewer than fifteen Iron Man Competitions, including the Iron Man World Championships in Kona, Hawaii in 2006. Balancing his role as a regional HR executive for a large multinational and family life, he also recently swam the lake in Zurich—all 26.5 kilometers (15 miles)! Stefan is a motivational and driven individual and his true passion—as his job title might suggest—is believing in others.

I asked Stefan about comfort zones and how important they are to get out of.

> **Stefan:** If you're comfortable to be average that's perfectly fine. But if you want to be more than average you've got to have a purpose in life.

Ryan: It sounds like from talking and knowing you that comfort zones aren't something that you stay in regularly. You actively push yourself out of comfort zones. Like learning how to swim and then challenging yourself to a big swimming event like that and going on to do Ironmans. If you stay average you can stay in your comfort zone. But if you want something better than that you push yourself out of that. Is that right?

Stefan: That is absolutely and totally right. If in life you're always asked the same questions you will always get the same answers. And nothing will change. It won't change for the better, and it won't change for the worst. It will just keep going as it is. Here again if you're happy with that, that's perfectly fine. But if you want to move things forward, if you want to get better in sports, if you want to get become better in what you do on a professional side, from time to time you need to take a risk. The risk as well involves the possibility that you will fail. My personal view is that I do not consider failure to be anything bad. I think failure is perfectly fine, but you need to learn from your mistakes. If you do that, that is perfectly fine.

Fear: 1-Ryan: 0 just after the first round. However, it's not going to win the next.

> *"The only thing we have to fear, is fear itself"*
> **—President Franklin D. Roosevelt**

WHAT IS FEAR?

> *"Fear is like getting mugged. All of sudden it jumps all over you, throws a few blows, steals your focus and leaves you dazed, anxious, apprehensive, confused and afraid to step out on your own anymore…only if you let it."*
> **—Ryan O'Reilly**

Fear is the mind creating anxiety about an event or experience that may or may not happen. It's the inner voice filling you full of doubt. It's what makes us stop doing something. It makes up the reasons and excuses why we "can not."

Are there different types of fear? Absolutely. This "mugger" takes many forms. It is a biological reaction from early mankind. Fight or Flight. It's what helped the human race survive. This is chemical, it is the same for everyone; it is how we human beings are built. We either run from the grizzly bear or fight it. We can't help feeling it, but we can certainly learn to recognize and deal with it better. Experience helps us here.

Karl Albrecht, Ph.D., wrote an article that appeared in *Psychology Today* in 2012. It was aptly titled "The (Only) Five Fears We Share." In the article he names the five fears as:

1. Fear of Extinction
2. Fear of Mutilation
3. Fear of Loss of Autonomy
4. Fear of Separation (fear of rejection)
5. Fear of Ego-Death (fear of failure)

1. Fear of Extinction

Albrecht says that fear of extinction is more than just the fear of dying. It is the fear of ceasing to exist. (Think of the fear of heights, standing on a bridge looking down!)

Honestly on that side of the bridge, looking down into a deep rushing ravine, all that you can probably think about is the potential or risk of dying. The adrenaline pumps through you because your body is preparing itself for what will happen next. I've had a fear of heights since I was young, adding to my fear of deep water.

2. Fear of Mutilation

Anxiety, he says, is about losing a part of us. The fear of mutilation is the fear of animals, spiders, snakes, or anything than cause us harm or damage our physical selves. Opening my apartment door one day in California on a glorious sunny day, there was a baby rattlesnake on our doorstep. Now for a native Californian, this might not have been a big deal, but for an Irish man whose patron saint (St. Patrick) drove all snakes from Ireland it was a bit of a shock. There was a little bit of fear, even though it was just a "baby rattler"

3. Fear of Loss of Autonomy

Also known as claustrophobia, he says, this fear is the fear of being restricted, overwhelmed, trapped, or being controlled by circumstances beyond our control. This happens in social and work situations all the time, right? I was overwhelmed in my last company and it was just getting too much. Trapped and controlled were two words that kept coming out of my situation for me, hence the need for a change of direction.

4. Fear of Separation

Albrecht calls this: Fear of abandonment, rejection, of becoming a non-person. Not wanted, or valued by anyone else. The people refusing to get into the same lift with me and taking the stairs was their way of telling me I wasn't wanted. I felt awful afterwards and now I know why. Fear of rejection made my self-worth decrease.

5. Fear of Ego-Death (Fear of Failure)

Finally, Albrecht states that the fear of our Ego-Death, or the fear of failure, is what grips us most often. This is the fear of humiliation, shame, and self-disapproval. He says it is the fear of shattering one's constructed sense of lovability, capability, and worthiness. I have feared failure, all my life and I now know why: my ego!

Knowing how it may sound that I tick all the boxes for each fear category is both personal sharing and refreshing for me. I bet you could think of a story for each category too.

DOES EVERYONE EXPERIENCE FEARS?

Yes. Simple answer. Show me a person who has no fear and I'll show you a person who is good at faking it. Internally they are using that fear and they are experiencing it just like you and me. Everyone experiences fear of some kind throughout their lives, as we are all human. The difference sometimes is how they choose to use fear to help them or how their drive is greater than their fears. Knowing what will surface in terms of fears for us, identifying it, and using our drive to move on is the key here. Recognize it, but don't bow to it. We need to understand how we can overcome it.

In October 2012, Felix Baumgartner, a daredevil of sorts, set the world record for skydiving. He dropped an estimated thirty-nine kilometers or twenty-four miles! It was an amazing scientific feat, not just a stunt. This was planned in advance for months, even years. Here's an interesting fact: Felix had to wear a special suit for the jump. It needed to be tight and restrictive for the endeavor he was about to partake in, which could have killed him. He became slightly overwhelmed with the suit. His sports psychologist was the famous Michael Gervais, who was the sports psychologist for the 2014 Super Bowl–winning Seattle Seahawks. The more Baumgartner thought of the restriction of the suit, the higher the anxiety levels went. He became wound up over the suit, threatening the whole project. Gervais was called in by the project team in a last ditch attempt to see if he could get into Felix's mind and fix the problem.

Gervais had to talk him around the fear of claustrophobia in the suit. He spent many weeks talking (over many sessions) to Felix. He talked about the fear and asked enough questions and took him through enough exercises for him to face the fear of the suit. It worked. He jumped. He survived. Imagine if he had let that fear get the better of him—it could have been fatal.

Fear is always there.

Susan Jeffers says there are a couple of truths relating to fear: "The fear will never go away as long as I continue to grow," and "Not only am I going to experience fear, whenever I'm on unfamiliar territory, so is everyone else."

So the mugger called fear is always there, and it's always there for everyone. Fact: If you want something in life, fear will try and jump on you. It comes down to how much you want to reach your goal, or how willing you are to fight for it. Fighting your fears and using them will help you master or at least control the speed of your travel toward your dreams.

Do not get derailed by your fears, but help yourself by recognizing them and bring them with you on the journey. Knowing what they are makes them feel less threatening, and knowing how we will react under given circumstances and use those reactions will help us.

I plan to retackle deep water, for example. It's not the water I am afraid of; it's the depth. Now that I know this, it's my new starting line. I want to get comfortable and skilled in deep water. Even thinking about it makes me get a chill! But imagine the exhilaration I will experience when I can master this fear. I'll open up more opportunities for myself in other areas of my life where I can be more confident. I'll hopefully be able to go and compete in an Iron Man endurance event. It will happen. I believe. I just need to beat the fear.

We fear that which we don't know or understand. If we understand it, we've already decided to face it. In relation to the depth of water, I've been watching YouTube videos of divers, of how to tread water, and am reading books about free-divers. This is all me trying to understand what it is that I fear.

Mahatma Gandhi wisely claimed:

The enemy is fear; we think it is hate, but it is really fear.

And Nelson Mandela on fear:

I learned that courage was not the absence of fear, but the triumph over it. The brave man is not he who does not feel afraid, but he who conquers that fear.

This is where drive comes in. The difference between successful and unsuccessful comes down to your own drive and focus on what you want.

I asked earlier in Chapter One: How badly do you want this? Are you really going to let anxiety and apprehension in the form of fear block you from achieving your goal or dream?

Susan Jeffers, author of *Feel the Fear and Do It Anyway: How to Turn Your Fear and Indecision into Confidence and Action,* inspired me to feel the fear of water and do it anyway. Even though I didn't beat the fear, I still tried. And that counts for something.

Here is an exercise to help you conquer fear:

1. Write down what it is that you fear.
2. Next, write down what the worst-case scenario could be if fear won.
3. List all the excuses and reasons you can't do something and come up with a way to creatively think of a way passed them.
4. Ask yourself how badly you want this.
5. Is your goal realistic? What small steps and small wins can help you get there?
6. What have you learned from your fears?
7. The old time management joke: How do you eat an elephant? One chunk at a time. Chunk it up. Make your goal more manageable and finally celebrate any success, no matter how small.
8. Winning over fear gives us confidence to face bigger and bolder challenges. Celebrate it. Own it. Conquer it.

THE NFL QUARTERBACK MIKE KAFKA

Mike is currently (at time of writing) the quarterback for the Minnesota Vikings in the National Football League (NFL). He was drafted by the Philadelphia Eagles and also spent time playing with New England Patriots and Tampa Bay Buccaneers. Mike played his college football career at Northwestern. Outside of football, Mike is also a budding entrepreneur and is CEO of his own sports and outdoor clothing company, *Roo Outdoors.*

I asked Mike was he always a driven individual. Mike gives some context for us on how professional sports people view drive. This view seems to be not so dissimilar to other professional sports people I have talked to.

You know what? I don't think I was. I think at some point—it probably was in high school—when I started getting really serious about sports and about training and about football. I had aspirations of initially just being one of the better players in my high school, one of the better players in my state at baseball or football. Those were the two main sports I played, so I really just wanted to be a good player and contribute to the team. Then as things started moving along I think, that drive kind of kicked in and I wanted to be a professional football player. Basically from high school I started just building and trying to figure out what the best guys are doing. How are they training? How are they studying? How are they doing these things? So I kind of built a plan to get to that level. The first step was being the best player in my state. Then it was going on to a college where I could play with the best. I went to Northwestern. When I went to Northwestern I had to play well there as well. So to be able to start games and play well and be in the team that they create. Then while being at Northwestern, the next step was to elevate my game to play in the NFL. Until then, I was lucky enough to have an opportunity with the Philadelphia Eagles. I was drafted in the fourth round and really from there, that's where the end goal was. Once I got to that end goal, I had to stay at that level, right?

In talking with Mike I found this interesting, that small steps—as outlined by Mike—lead to big success. Every milestone Mike reached was just a part of a bigger picture. Let us all agree that to get to be an NFL quarterback level is probably one of the more competitive areas of sport and life, but Mike looked at it as a progression; a next step. I took the opportunity to ask Mike also about fear. We look at American football and see—as sports viewers—confident players. What's a quarterback's point of view?

Fear is really nothing. It's your brain telling you what possibly could happen, like what could possibly go wrong. There's definitely a difference between fear and danger, right? Danger is a grizzly bear right in front of you ready to take your head off, right? That's danger. But fear is while walking through the woods I could possibly run into a grizzly bear. You know what I mean? That's fear to me. Fear is essentially you making up something that could possibly happen, when in fact it hasn't happened yet.

I decided to ask about "fear" in professional sports stars. Is fear ever present?

Absolutely. I think it's human nature for that to cross your mind. But some people are able to take that fear and turn it around and use it for motivation to play better. I think it just depends on how you can deal with that or deal with those emotions and it's all about managing those emotions.

In the next chapter, we talk about potential and self-worth. Potentially the best chapter yet!

CHAPTER 4

POTENTIAL

The Harvard students passed by me in droves. These well-educated and mostly wealthy students wore the best clothes and study at one of the best, most expensive, and well-known universities in the world. It was 1996.

They all laughed and seemed in control, and to be honest, I felt a little intimidated. I sat there at my desk. My security badge was pinned to my white security issue shirt. The walkie-talkie crackled the normal security officer chat. Lauryn Hill and the Fugees were "killing me softly" in the background on the radio. The fan at my feet cooled me as a new form of never-before-experienced-eastern-humidity hit me.

I checked the identification as the students entered The Harvard Vanderbilt residency halls. This was my first time living in the driven country that is the United States. I was determined to get there and left Ireland on my own to take a summer job at nineteen. My first job in the USA was painting houses. Being a security guard was my second. I worked as a security guard around the Harvard Business and Medical Schools campus. I would pull an eight-hour shift in the Vanderbilt residence hall then put another eight hour shift in one of the Harvard research buildings off the Longwood campus. I worked sixteen hours a day, six days a week, on $6.25 an hour. It was a grueling, but super experience.

I learned what potential was all about. Kids who weren't much older than me, were there to become doctors, lawyers, or scientists. There was an air of positivity in the place, an optimism. They believed in where they were going. At the time, I knew the direction to the airport home to Ireland—that was about it.

Even though my confidence had taken a huge leap forward, I still felt intimidated. I realized my ambitions had to be greater. Having finished my first year of University, I was seriously thinking about not continuing with college and instead maybe joining the police force in Ireland. Watching these Harvard students full of potential, I knew I was aiming too low. I knew I could do better for myself. On my security checks, I used to stand on the roof of one of the tallest buildings and watch the sun rise to the east. This used to lift my spirits to no end, knowing I was standing on top of a Harvard building, looking out over the Boston skyline as the sun greeted me with its warm summer early glow.

One evening I was checking IDs. My shift was nearly over and the students seemed to be passing through the doors in small numbers now.

The rule was no ID, no entry. Everyone was polite and friendly and some stopped for a quick chat.

One kid came in—a rich kid with a rich attitude. He went to open the security door.

"Hey man, open the door!"

"Hi, can I see your ID please?"

"Just open the door, you dick!"

"Well, I need to see your ID."

"Listen, you asshole, I have an important assignment. I'm a student here at Harvard. You're a security guard, which is more important? Open the damn door."

I opened the door. (Not before whispering, "Prick!" under my breath.)

This guy who had been randomly standing next in line, walked up to me. He was unassuming and seemed just like all the other decent students.

"Hey what's your name, man?"

"Ryan" I told him, still red faced and embarrassed from the abuse from the rich kid.

"Ryan, let me give you some advice. Anyone talks to you like that again, you look them square in the eye and you remember what they say and you go and prove them wrong. That guy was an asshole. You're not just a security guard—you're a guy that's going to prove him wrong, right?"

I nodded and thanked him. I wasn't sure why he said it, but it was a kind gesture.

Later in my travel journal I wrote down what he said. But I focused in on a few things and underlined them.

I was going to prove them wrong. "Them" wasn't the rich kid. It was a collection of all the people who hadn't backed me or had underestimated me or assumed that I'd never amount to much.

That night I also wrote—*My potential is only limited by me.* I believed it.

So, I made it my mission over the next few years to keep improving and keep going forward. Progression, I thought, would help me with potential. People like that guy at the door are everywhere and I've learned to deal with them better. I might not always tell them I'll prove them wrong, but if someone underestimates me or my potential, I make it a big personal goal to try prove him or her wrong.

I like to refer to it as a "positive" chip on my shoulder. Sometimes it is that chip that completely motivates me.

That summer as a security guard remained in the back of my mind. I went on to finish University and developed a passion for commerce and business. I also started believing in other's potential. I started telling people I did. The difference a few simple words can make to someone is unbelievable. I've even sat down with some senior leaders and backed them. Everyone needs a supporter.

To be told that someone believes in you and your potential is a special thing. So I became a believer in people's potential, even if they didn't see it. Out of all these experiences, I firmly believe in everyone. Anyone has the potential to make a better life for themselves, to reach their dreams. They just have to reach.

The question is are you proving them wrong, and if not, when are you going to start?

I've been lucky. I can count on some choice moments and some stellar individuals who believed in me and in my potential. Not only believed in it but also backed me and mentored me to achieve all that I could.

I've also traveled and learned from different cultures. It is enthralling to work in a different country; the insights can be really eye opening.

Add to that a job in sales management, where one could argue everything is about potential. Managing salespeople with low confidence and low interest but with huge potential is tough. Leading people with high confidence and high potential can be easier than leading people with low confidence and low drive. Once a team is confident of it's potential the limits start to be redefined and shattered. A team that underestimates each other is a team doomed to not reach its potential. The same goes for individuals.

When I was younger, people used to underestimate me all the time. I think my external self-confidence was so low that people probably thought I wouldn't amount to much. At such a young age, I was worried that I'd never have any potential, and that fear drove me to be competitive and try to live a better life.

Through school and university (and you could argue work) I built up this external veneer of confidence. At times, folks would see it as cockiness, other times as confidence. I was trying to show the world that I could make something of myself, on my own and without fear. I was careful not to show any vulnerability, and be focused and unrelenting.

People underestimating me used to make me quietly determined. I didn't want the world to underestimate me or to judge my potential. I didn't want anyone to put me in a box or dismiss my chances. My silent mission was to try and prove people wrong. Today, if you tell me I can't do something, I'm going to try it just to prove you wrong. If it's something I want to do, I'll do it and won't tell you till I've either completed it or I'm ready to kick it.

"The potential of the average person is like a huge ocean un-sailed, a new continent unexplored, a world of possibilities waiting to be released and channeled toward some great good."

—Brian Tracy

"Potential is the difference between where you are now and where you could be after removing your self-imposed limits!"
> —**Ryan O'Reilly**

"My potential is only limited by me."
> —**Ryan O'Reilly**

HOW IS POTENTIAL RELATED TO SELF-WORTH?

Potential is a curious thing. It really does come down to self-belief and self-worth. One of my favorite books is Tony Robbins' *Awaken the Giant Within*.

If you haven't heard of him, Tony Robbins is the leading empowerment speaker in the world. Why? He believed in his own potential and the potential of others. He teaches people how to believe in themselves and awaken the giant inside each of us.

Self-worth is so important in trying to reach our potential. In my last corporate job before I started my own business, my self-worth had reached an all-time low. On a scale of one to ten I was below zero. I felt like I was something on my old boss' shoe. Partly, it was my own fault because I let others demean me in meetings and emails. I was becoming like the people I didn't want to be anymore.

There were dark days when I couldn't see the future. I would berate myself for being useless; I would get very down on myself. Anything that went wrong would make me chip away at my own self-worth. My potential for success was now hampered. My mental strength was waning, before it was formidable. Previously my bounce-back ability was strong. But this was knocking the wind out of my sails. I was nervous about where I was going. No-where-ville wasn't a place I wanted to land. I kept wondering:

- How are things going to pan out?
- Will I be able to pay the bills?
- Was I making the right decision?
- Who would employ me as a sales trainer?

I started to re-read books that had given me a huge lift earlier in my life.

Rocket Boys by Homer Hickman Jr. was a great book about potential. For those of you who haven't read it, it's about a group of boys who want to build rockets. They start off really small and improve all the time. They become passionate about a rocket and its potential. They go from small amateur rockets to something bigger every time they build. Some of the boys even ended up working for NASA. The book's theme is that anything is possible.

And another book was that of Roger Bannister.

In 1954, Roger Bannister ran the first sub-four minute mile. He believed in his potential and human potential to break through pre-thought limits. He did it and always believed in himself to get there. Once he had ran a sub-four mile, there was a watershed. In America, this year alone, hundreds of college athletes will break the four minutes. Imagine how many break it across the world. Bannister showed the way, and he helped us think beyond what we thought possible. He broke the limit for us, and because of that many aren't afraid now to go for it.

IS OUR POTENTIAL LIMITLESS?

No, it isn't. Everyone's *physical* potential is different. I can't run sub-four minutes, for example. I'm just not fast enough. (Although not from lack of trying!) However in life and business, I believe there is a limitless internal potential of how much we can grow and develop ourselves. If our focus is always about chasing our own potential then we'll always be moving forward. Small steps lead to big success when it comes to potential.

Potential and drive are very closely related. In my opinion, you cannot have one without the other. If you are described as a driven person, or a person who is goal driven, then you're stepping toward your potential a little closer each day.

If you are told you have potential and the words underused or untapped have been used to describe you, then maybe what is missing is a bit of drive.

HOW DO WE DRIVE OURSELVES TO REACH OUR POTENTIAL?

1. Goal Setting

Goal setting is a great way to start building your potential. If you set goals regularly and achieve them, then that's a good sign you're driving forward.

If you set goals that seem to be always out of reach or never realize themselves, then maybe start by setting some that are more achievable to you.

Exercise

Write down seven life goals.

When the list is complete, review and then pick one goal of the seven.

Focus on this one goal and do one thing daily that will get you on the road to achieving that goal. Nothing can stop you.

For example, if one of your life goals is to run a marathon, then your daily activity is to run. After fifteen days start setting down a plan to tackle the bigger parts of the goal. After two weeks of running, maybe sign up to a running group or start a training plan to get you there. Do something every day to get you closer to your goal until it's so clear and in sight that you can see it actually happening.

2. Learn from Others

There are heroes everywhere. Heroes are people with huge potential who have done amazing feats throughout their lives. Study these people or read their autobiographies. Go to motivational seminars where the best speak about human potential and about crushing limits. Look to your network of family and friends. I bet you will find someone who believes in potential and has a good story to tell.

3. Invest in Yourself

How much potential do you have? Only you know. To master your area of expertise or an area that inspires you, invest yourself in learning as much as you can about the topic. If it's too expensive, save for it. If saving is not possible, then how important is your potential to you? Remember, nothing should stop you from reaching your full potential. Find a way. If you're finding it hard to figure it out, seek some guidance from someone who is driven and has lived up to his or her own potential. Brainstorm it with them. Hire a business or life coach.

4. Understand What Your Fears and Limits Are

Write them down. Mine are the fear of drowning and the fear of not being good enough.

Once you know what they are, then start focusing on possible ways to overcome them and help yourself release your own potential. Feel that fear!

5. Take Time to Reflect on How Far You Have Come and How Much Further You Want to Go

Get a quiet place to sit and reflect. Reflect on your journey so far, is there anything you can learn from, etc. Write down they key things you have learned.

6. Believe in Yourself

If you don't believe in yourself, who will? Who believed in Mark Zuckerberg, Steve Jobs, Bill Gates, Tim Cook, and Roger Bannister? They believed in themselves, were true to their own ideals and values, and didn't put limits on their own or their companies' potential.

It's normal to have doubts. Everyone has them. They are the part of us that wants us to stay safe and comfortable. Don't waste time getting into a circle of doubt. Can you try and write down what types of doubts come up most often?

You probably have a pattern—there is going to be a trigger. Can you write down when something or someone triggers these doubts? Triggers are something that set off that thinking of doubt or self-doubt. We think too much sometimes, don't we?

Is there one person who believes in you no matter what you do? Your kids? A teacher? A coach? For my clients, that's what I do. I am the person that believes in them 100 percent. I'm the cheerleader.

Unwavering belief that you can be whatever you want to be is the best way to live up to your potential. Learn everyday. You need to become focused on believing. If you believe strongly enough in yourself and your own potential, then there are no limits. Though, hard work has no substitute. It really is how much you believe in yourself and how you will unshackle those self-imposed limits.

Albert Einstein said, "I am thankful to all those who said no. It's because of them I did it myself."

It was a rainy day. All the early morning commuters were rushing under umbrellas and grabbed take away coffees as they walked. I was sitting inside a little café and the rain was only inches away. The café was one that didn't have a front door. I jumped in there, as I was early and wanted refuge from the rain. There was a homeless man hunkered under a large, plastic sheet outside the door. He was huddled beside a phone box. He looked tired and hungry. I noticed he was holding a book. I couldn't see the title. I jumped from my seat, ordered a large tea to go, and as I was waiting for the barista to fulfill my order, I wrote a note on a small Post-it.

I walked out in the rain and made eye contact with the man who happened to have no home. I handed him the hot cup of tea and the note in the hand that was holding the book. He opened the note and read it. I smiled at him. He smiled back. I went back to my seat inside the door.

The note said, "It's raining today. It'll be sunny tomorrow. Believe in your own potential."

I don't know if it helped or why I did it. I just felt I needed to say something to him without embarrassing him. I have no idea what happened next. But I have to believe it might have lifted his spirits that day. Under the deluge of rain and the plastic sheet, for a brief minute drinking tea—maybe he believed in the future, too.

Believe in your own potential. Prove "them" wrong. Enjoy it when you do!

We've got to believe it will be sunny tomorrow. You can do it. I believe in you, and I've probably never met you. But you're reading this book, so I know you are interested in reaching your potential. I named my company High Potential International because I believe in everyone's unlimited high potential.

"Life's battles don't always go to the stronger or the faster man, but sooner or later the man who wins is the man who says he can."

—From the poem "The Man Who Thinks He Can" by **Walter D. Wintle**

THE HIGH PERFORMANCE DIRECTOR ON THE UNITED STATES OLYMPIC COMMITTEE, FIN KIRWAN

Fin Kirwan works as a high-performance director on the United States Olympic Committee. Fin is responsible for leading teams of sports experts in supporting Olympic high performance programs in track and field, swimming, equestrian, shooting and weightlifting.

An interesting discussion with Fin Kirwan helped me understand the mindset and viewpoints on drive from someone who works closely with Olympic athletes. Before he was on the Olympic Committee, Fin was a member of the highly successful, high performing Irish Boxing Olympic team for the Irish Sports Council. I asked Fin about an Olympian's drive and what it means for them.

Fin: Certainly in Olympic athletes I think they are really focused on the next competition and focused on making the Olympic team and don't necessarily see beyond that. And then you've got other athletes who are more experienced and have possibly won Olympic medals and are driven by a much broader thing about their legacy and being seen to succeed at the highest level. So, I think from an athlete's perspective it depends very much on the phase of their career that they're going through. Some of them, certainly in the sports like track and field, some of the events—like men's/women's 100, men's/women's short hurdles, long hurdles, 110 hurdles or 400 hurdles—they're so deep here that the drive for a lot of college kids really is just to make the national team and that in itself is a very difficult thing to do. So there are several different ways of looking at it. For me personally, I think I'm driven by the fact that I came from originally a business background and I'm driven really by helping our athletes get better."

Even now, listening back to the podcast, I really liked Fin's answer. Not because it gave me insight into Olympians, but because it could be true for you and me. (The full podcast and interview with Fin are available on www.ryanoreillyinternational.com.) I also asked him what he thought the link was between elite performance and potential. Fin stated:

I think everybody's got potential. This is what I really honestly think. Literally everybody's got potential. There's a coach—I'm trying to remember his name—Arthur Lydiate. He coached Peter Snell to the Olympic gold medal in 800 meters in Rome in 1960. And Arthur said "there's an Olympian in every village." And the point being that there's potential everywhere. You know you can look around anywhere and you'll find people who are good enough to succeed and have the ability and the talent. But what they don't have is the drive and the passion and the commitment to do what's needed to fulfill the potential. And that for me—now involved in high-performance sport for about thirteen years—the defining characteristic for me is potential and talent combined with work ethic. If you don't have the work ethic—so if you can't handle the three-a-day training sessions in swimming here—there's no point. You may as well just go home and you'll be told to go home. Because there are ten other guys who want that spot who will do the three-a-days. So I think potential—you won't go anywhere without it—but without potential and talent (but equally potential and talent) are nothing without work ethic and that would be my view. And I saw that it doesn't matter if it's Michael Phelps, Missy Franklin or you know, Katie Taylor. It's the same. Each one of them have enormous levels of talent but more important, probably on top of that that they've got incredible work ethic. And that work ethic then allows them to really maximize their potential. I had the pleasure of spending quite a bit of time with Katie Taylor leading into the London Olympics in 2012 and she is as driven, she's quite a humble person but there's nobody with a greater work ethic than her. And people presume she was going to win the gold medal, people presume she was always going to win her next fight but the reality was that she was preparing, the only way that was happening was because of the quality of her preparation.

In the next chapter, we talk about skill and aptitude. Now, if you would be so kind as to skillfully turn the page!

CHAPTER 5

SKILL AND APTITUDE

W hen I was younger, I played rugby football in school and for a short while after. It was absolutely super to be part of a competitive team, and it really taught me some valuable life lessons. Being a shy and self-conscious, tall teenager who was incredibly light for such a physically demanding game, made it difficult for me to assert any influence on the games. It was hard for me to be good at the sport, not that I didn't want to be good. I wrote myself off because I felt I didn't have the skill or aptitude for the game. I was a late starter, too light, and didn't have enough knowledge of the rules were all the excuses I told myself. Self-doubt overcame me every time I togged out. I was well outside my comfort zone. I wasn't aggressive enough. I made excuses, but I still worked hard at showing up to train and tried to learn more.

In my first year playing rugby, we reached the finals for our provincial inter-schools competition. It was a big deal for us. We were going to be junior cup champions. The team was packed with skillful and talented lads, and competition for places was tough. I was hanging onto the squad by the skin of my teeth.

Rugby fields fifteen, and six substitutes only, bringing it to a total of twenty-one. In that junior year I was always number twenty-one. Super Sub! Water boy references all welcome!

As the team was being named for the upcoming semi-final, it was a huge occasion for the school. I got dropped from the team. I hadn't missed training or a game all year. Someone else jumped in to the twenty-first spot, and that was it. I was cut from the team. It stung a little, particularly when some of my teammates goaded me over it—as fifteen-year-olds will do. Maybe they didn't realize how important it was for me to be part of the team.

The next training session before the big semi-final, the squad made their way out to the backfield at the school. I waited until they all left the dressing room, then went down and changed into my sports gear. The day was wet. The field we trained on was part of a four-field set-up. I didn't go to training with the team. I ran the perimeter of the fields one lap after another. I kept running around and around. A teacher, who knew I had been dropped and who happened to be out walking called out to me, "You show them Ryan!"

The same teacher had been an Olympic coach. It meant a lot. I kept running, and was gone from the dressing room before my teammates returned. My rugby coaches saw me running. So did the team.

Of course the team won the semi-final. They were a talented group, and they had a desire to win the cup. I was in the crowd, cheering them on as loudly as my classmates.

The following week was the final. The person who replaced me had a dispute with the coach over something and left the team.

I was back in! I was number 21 for the final match!

On the bus that day, one of our teachers and coaches, Father Frank O'Connor, called me to where he was seated on the bus. He said, "Ryan, your name isn't on the match day program." He explained that they hadn't time to change it before printing. Even though I was on the team, my name was not matching the slot number in the three-page program.

I looked him in the eye and said, "Father, being here and being part of this day is more important to me than my name on any program. Thanks for letting me be a part of it."

We lost by three points in the last minutes of the game. I never played a minute. But I felt part of it. I knew everyone was more skillful than me, but I will never forget the lessons that I learned that year.

Rugby football is a game of confidence as much as it is a game of skill. Years later when my confidence grew, I was in my final year of University in the United Kingdom. A few of us were asked to tog out for the local team. It was a third team selection, nothing too serious. Before the game in the afternoon, I sat in my student dorm room and psyched myself up. I wanted to make up for my lack of skill with passion. I was going to be the most passionate on the pitch, committed to every tackle. I was going to fire my team up by the way I played.

It worked.

I believed so much in my ability to be passionate that my skills weren't of concern to me during the game. Then it happened. This belief had me run down a kick that was caught by their last man. He tried to field and kick the ball away but I was so hyped up I blocked the kick, gathered the ball, and ran twenty yards beneath the posts for a try (rugby's touchdown)!

Twenty-two years later, I was back in my hometown for a birthday celebration, and my wife booked us into a hotel in the city of my birth for a nice meal and an evening away from the kids. The next morning, at 7 a.m. I got my running gear on and headed out of the hotel entrance. I ran in the mild December air for about four miles until I got to my old school, St. Munchin's College Limerick. The school still has a wonderful building and grounds. The school of course had been remodeled since I went to school and looked more modern, but still had the same old charm.

The gates were closed to the large old boarding school. I ran around the side of the school and down by the adjoining river. I hopped the fence into the school grounds and ran parallel to the building until I was at the back of it and stood on the four pitches. I breathed in and closed my eyes. It was still the same; still magical in its own way. There were so many happy memories.

Beginning to run again, I made my way slowly around the perimeter of the four adjoining fields—the same one I did on my own all those years ago. As I progressed in the run, nostalgia and a sense of gratitude overcame me. I had come a long way from that day getting dropped from the team and having to show how driven I was to be involved by running this lap. Lots had happened since. I realized I was a man (and a father!) running the lap now, and the last time I was just a boy—a boy with dreams to be involved and to be part of something bigger than himself. The man still had dreams, just with a different perspective now. Running back to the hotel, I couldn't help but smile. I had mud splattered legs from "the first year mile"- the circumference of the four football pitches- as it's called at the school. My head was lighter for the experience, making many different types of teams since and thankful for the journey and what that lesson taught me.

> *"It is your attitude, not your aptitude that will determine your altitude."*
> **—Zig Ziglar**

> *"Skill and aptitude are the parts that will help you drive faster. However, if your will is greater than your skill you will accelerate."*
> **—Ryan O'Reilly**

My point here is this, if you're passionate about being good at something, or even just becoming better, it not only helps, but it might get you over the line. Others might not think you have the skills or the potential. My rugby story only served me in the other parts of my life. From then on I wanted to make the team, skilled or not. Everything I did after drove me to make the team and to be on that special project group or senior management team, I wanted to be on the field of play.

DO YOU THINK YOU DON'T HAVE ENOUGH SKILL?

Get a Mentor

Skill levels can vary from person to person and from task to task. If we think we don't have enough, then we need to understand what it will take to get better. Get a good mentor and understand how long it took them to master this particular skill.

How do I find a mentor? How much do they cost?

Sometimes, mentors can be available at your place of work. In large businesses there are usually mentor programs that pair up mentors and mentees. In fact, if you think there are no mentors available to you, just step back and take a look around. Often neighbors, friends of friends, or relations can fill the shoes of a good mentor. We have to be open to the potential of mentors entering our lives where we least expect them and open to having many rather than just one.

Retrain

Is there a course or professional group that can help you get better at the skill? How will you master it?

Join a group, seek out the experts who have the skills. Ask them questions.

One of my coaching clients told me the other day, "I don't have the skills, and it would be too hard." This particular person was hiding behind her lack of skills as the reason why she couldn't do something. We're all guilty of that to some degree, aren't we? I know I personally feel like this all the time. Skills are learnable. The trick is to retrain, not just our skills, but also our mindsets. How do we do this? Well that's what this book is about—it's all down to how we reach into our own drive and create the mindset for realizing our potential.

Cultivate a Great Attitude

Believe that you can learn or get past any obstacle. You do need a certain skill set to be successful and fine tuning those skills will help you in the long run. But, realize that attitude can carry you a long way.

Get Hungry!

I've asked this of you a few times now. How badly do you want it?

Hunger is unquantifiable. But it is the difference between success and failure. Self-talk and self-doubt all eat away at the hunger. Are you focused 100 percent on your dream or your goal? Skills and aptitude will not get you there every time. Be hungry for the goal you want to achieve.

Play to Your Strengths

Small daily improvements in your habits, and small steps forward will help you become successful. Play to your strengths. It goes back to eating that elephant: taking small bites every day will get you motivated.

Focus on the Basics

Do you think athletes or business executives try new things every day? They all focus on the basics and do the basics super well. If you can execute the basics of your job, become known for executing them excellently. Six months down the road, people will start to recognize your execution at the basics. For example, in sales the basics are asking good questions and understanding the customer. If you become great at those two things, you will be successful and people will notice.

Skills Are Important

Lack of skill will only get you so far, however attitude can help you compensate and win more. The people who are most successful in life hold the same positivity in attitude and "can do" is something inherent to them.

Remember there will always be people who are faster, stronger, or more capable than you. It's the law of the jungle. Isn't that part of the allure for people like you and me? We want it more, and sometimes that's all we need to be driven, achieve, and win!

It's all about marching to develop ourselves to be better. And with that said, let's march together to the next chapter which is on self-development!

CHAPTER 6

SELF-DEVELOPMENT

When I was fifteen, I got my first paid job. When I say paid job, I mean employment from someone other than my parents. I needed a job, I needed money, and I wanted to start building my employability factor by collecting good references. At fifteen, part-time jobs can be difficult to find. I walked the length of my hometown and asked every business for work. We weren't a wealthy family, and my parents worked extremely hard just making ends meet. This job was my way of becoming independent, of being able to buy my own clothes, or music, or books without relying on an allowance. I needed a job badly; it was almost a matter of survival for me.

These business owners all asked me the same questions: What can you do? (I didn't know.) What experience do you have? (I hadn't much.) I remember thinking all I needed was a start. But how do you get that start?

Eventually after visiting the same places twice over two days, I encountered a lady who had met me briefly the day before. She was a hotel hiring manager.

I had repeated the same question I had asked the day before. "Is there any job going that I could do part time?"

She smiled. "Weren't you here yesterday?"

Yes, I explained that I was trying everyone again in case something had changed. Naïve, I know! She took my home phone number again and repeated what she had told me yesterday. "Nothing at the moment, we'll call you."

I said thanks, and then said, "By the way, I am a hard worker. I won't let you down." And I meant it.

A few days later, I got a call from one of the other hotel managers at the same hotel. I was still in school. It was mid week and the guy explained they needed me for a few hours for an important job, I'd be home before 11 p.m., and it would be a bit of money. I had to ask my mother, but as soon as I did and she approved, I practically ran to the hotel.

The important job was washing pots and pans and hotel dishes. It was a massive hotel kitchen, with steam and heat. The sinks were larger than anything I had ever seen. And man, it was noisy! Not to mention the heat from the head chef as he roared at his assistant chefs and the waiting staff to execute on the service.

The dishwashing area was tiny and was surrounded by large shelves and spaces where cups, saucers, plates, pots, and pans could be placed for easy retrieval. It paid £2 an hour (approximately $1.75—hey, it was 1992!). Over the next six months, I worked eighteen hours every weekend—7 a.m. to 4 p.m. on Saturday and Sunday. During the week I had school and rugby. In the summer, when all my friends were heading to France or Austria to learn languages, I was working fifty to sixty hours a week washing pots and pans. It was tough work, but true to my promise I didn't let them down. I worked harder than anyone in the dishwashing department. Every day I'd figure out what else I could to do to impress. I always showed up early, never missed a day, and if they said jump, I'd jump twice as far.

If a pot came in that was covered in burns or the food it cooked was welded to the end of it. I'd make it my day's mission to get it spotless. Pretty soon, I became an expert dishwasher. Not many people have this on their resume. Even today, when there is a nasty-looking, everyone-ignoring-saucepan at home, I am the one who takes it and gets it clean. It brings me back and reminds me how far I have come in twenty years. I am still a dishwasher—just a dishwasher who's achieved a bit more than most.

WHAT HAS DISHWASHING GOT TO DO WITH SELF-DEVELOPMENT?

For me, those months took my inherited hard work ethic and leaped it forward a notch. With steam hitting my face and the stench of leftover food, I began to focus my mind on what I wanted to do in life. I now had a greater appreciation for what hard work was. No matter where I ended up in life, I had done one of the hardest and least desirable of jobs. And I had done it well. Wherever I ended up, it would have to be better than dish and pan washing! I dreamt of a nine-to-five office job. I imagined being able to get dressed in a suit and just talk to people all day long. Compared to dishwashing, it sounded like heaven.

That job also gave me a huge appreciation for people. Being the dishwasher in a hotel wasn't the most glamorous job the hotel offered. In fact, it was the worst. Chefs would shout at us; waiters and waitresses would take their own frustrations out on us if the cups weren't stacked right or there were no plates. We'd get the brunt of it. Sounds like a lot like modern day corporate life, doesn't it?

At such a young age, it made an impression. I learned to always treat people well, no matter who they are. Have respect for them. Something I have always tried to achieve in all my interactions with people, whether they are senior vice presidents of large corporate enterprises or homeless people on the street. I also learned to believe in people. Remember I was the youngest on staff, but there were plenty of high school dropouts that were working full time at the ages of sixteen or seventeen. I took an interest in these people. Every now and again, one of them would come to me for advice on a course they were starting or a new job they were applying for. Self-development became the theme; even at a young age, I was recommending books for people to read. That experience helped me develop myself, just like being dropped by the rugby team helped me forge tenacity and drive to self-improve daily.

That job also helped me pay for my first trip outside of Ireland. The long summer hours washing pots and pans helped me pay for my school's mid-term trip to France. We spent a day at the Normandy landing beaches, and we went to Paris. It was a reward that helped me develop further and broaden my mind. Standing on the beaches at Normandy, breathing in that fresh air, I realized how lucky I was, and how grateful I was for those thousands of soldiers who died there.

Even during those long days hunkered over a large sink, I knew that I was developing myself. Character building, so to speak. I felt it and used it as motivation for every pan, cup, and saucer that I cleaned. For every floor I mopped or grill I scrubbed, I notched up more tenacity, more work ethic, more *grit*. I'd play mental math games to keep myself sane. I'd benchmark myself versus my peers, and see if I could secretly be better. I could feel myself getting more confident in my work. My pain threshold for thirteen-hour shifts increased, and cleaning bins helped me develop myself into a harder worker . It's how I have looked at every job since. The key lesson I took away was that I learned to like the job. I mastered the machinery, the sinks, and the role. It was a great lesson all for $1.75 an hour!

Every job after that first, I asked the same questions every day. You can ask yourself the same ones:

- How am I moving here?
- What am I learning?
- What would I do differently?
- How can I learn from this?
- How can I master this role? (Be it washing dishes or delivering $100M in sales revenue through 120 people.)
- What are the bad parts of the job, and how do I get them done quickly and efficiently?
- What are the good parts of the job? (Like when the head chef would only come to me to clean an expensive pot.)

Later when I was managing large teams of salespeople, I asked:

- How can I impart some of my learning and experience?
- How can I motivate the people in junior positions? (Like me as the dishwasher.)
- Who can I help do their jobs better? (The waiters and waitresses.)

Self-Development is massively important for success. Small details, big impact.

At the end of your life, are you going to be able to say you gave it everything and developed as a person or are you going to be stuck in the past and be full of regret? Self-development is all about moving forward.

> *"There is nothing noble in being superior to your fellow man; true nobility is being superior to your former self."*
> **—Ernest Hemingway**

> *"If the you of last year, the you of this year, and the you of next year all interviewed for a job. Which one of "you" would get the contract? YOU are your own competition in life. Make the you of tomorrow better than the you of today."*
> **—Ryan O'Reilly**

The year I left that last corporate job, I was stuck and self-development was tough. I had to hold a mirror to myself and be more self-aware. What I saw, I didn't like. I was bitter and angry. I was failing at most relationships and I nearly self-destructed. It was a tough year, but sometimes when it's tough and there is failure, the lessons are monumental. Thanks to those people who at the time seemed to enjoy being my enemies, I developed my self-esteem and my confidence. It made me better, more resilient when my mental toughness was waning. It made me rediscover the true me.

My story might be different to yours or there might be plenty of similarities. I was stuck in a bad job and I thought there were no other options. But aren't we all just trying to get better and develop ourselves more? We're all trying to move forward, aren't we?

We develop if we:

- Constantly push ourselves from our comfort pits.
- Strive to be better than we were yesterday.
- Learn from our mistakes.
- Celebrate our successes without dwelling on them.

Driven people constantly push themselves from their comfort zones/pits. It's the small steps here that help us become better people, better leaders, better husbands/fathers, wives/mothers, and partners.

Drive is all about moving forward. It is all about self-development and creating the YOU of tomorrow. If we develop ourselves through reading, meditation, mindfulness, or just by listening more, we are putting our old selves out of business.

HAVE YOU ALWAYS TRIED TO DEVELOP YOURSELF?

I am a firm believer in making small steps and changing all the time. When you get better, more opportunities open themselves to you. Your viewpoints change and new people and conversations happen. Read to improve and strive to learn about yourself.

When writing down my life goals some years ago I scribbled: "write a book." Hands up—who has done that at one stage? I always knew I'd write one. But "maybe next year" excuses or something else would get in the way. That was my old self. To reach my goal, I had to stop making excuses, and start moving forward.

PUT YOUR OLD SELF OUT OF BUSINESS

Malcolm Gladwell, in his excellent book *Outliers,* discusses the 10,000-hour rule. He says that self-development has a tipping point. If you put in 10,000 hours of practice in any given subject, you will master that topic.

How many of us put 10,000 hours into developing ourselves or are consciously having focus during our practice to get better?

The aim should be to always put our "old" selves out of business. Whether it's earning that degree or going back to school, losing some weight, taking up a new activity, or getting a new job or new career. Forging a new version of us is the priority.

Have you ever met a relative or an old friend after a few years and they have said to you things like:

"You have changed an awful lot!"

"You've done so much."

"You've lost so much weight."

That is due to the fact that the "You" they met a year ago or longer is different than the "You" they meet now. We change whether we know it consciously or unconsciously.

WHEN DO YOU STOP SELF-DEVELOPING AND START DOING?

Great question. I have two answers.

First, you should never stop developing yourself; there is always a small amount of learning that can be done from daily interactions with people, bosses, or peers. This is where the real gold lies. Keeping a journal will help you track these lessons and observations. By the way, it's not your boss' or superior's job to develop you. It belongs to you. Own it.

Keeping a journal will also help you identify and learn from setbacks. Podcasts, audio books, print books, and YouTube are all so easily accessible. With the advent of websites like Ted.com (an online speaker series about ideas), it is possible to learn something new when you're on the move, or even just five minutes in the evening.

Second, the "start doing" part is vital. This is drive coming in, again. Developing YOU means getting stuff done! It means taking small steps daily to become a better person, whether that means mastering the excel sheet that you've been fighting with or having better conversations. For me, it's about being the best coach and motivational speaker I can be. What is it for you?

With the old model of "ready, aim, fire," it's easy to spend an inordinate amount of time planning. Instead, try a ready, fire, and then re-aim approach. This means taking a small action while still in planning or ready mode. Don't overcook the planning part. Start taking action. Remember, small steps lead to big success. A small step each day will add up over a month or a year.

Put yourself of yesterday out of business today.

THE NEW YORK TIMES BEST SELLING AUTHOR, MARK C. THOMPSON

Mark C. Thompson is a New York Times Best Selling Author, whose books include *ADMIRED: 21 Ways to Double Your Value, Now Build a Great Business*, and *Success Built to Last—Creating a Life that Matters*. Mark is also an Innovation Leadership columnist for Forbes.com, Inc.com and FastCompany.com. His most recent bestseller *ADMIRED* is a primer on how the world's "most admired companies" achieve long-term success and growth as well as the qualities that are common to "most admired leaders."

Mark has worked side by side as an executive coach with three of the world's most legendary disruptive innovators: Steve Jobs, Charles Schwab, and Virgin Group founder Sir Richard Branson. Forbes called Mark one of America's Top Venture Investors with the "Midas touch.". The American Management Association recently featured Mark as one of the world's top executive coaches and number one thought leader on innovation and engagement. He was also named one of the "Top 30 Communications Professionals for 2015" by Global Gurus. Mark advises top leaders in Fortune 500 and Global Fortune 1000 companies as well as the executive teams who are leading high growth startup companies in Silicon Valley today. Mark is one of the most in-demand executive coaches in the world. Mark very kindly gave up some of his valuable time to be interviewed for this book. I took the opportunity to ask Mark how people who feel stuck in neutral can self-develop themselves to move on and reach their true potential.

> **Mark:** I'd say that the mastery that comes with pursuing that drive would be to do three things really well. We saw this with all the people who are high achievers, and that was to first, think about where are the gaps in the skillsets that are necessary for the very best people at that task. Anyone who's ever gone out

and interviewed the top achievers in any field usually learns what are the skills and sensibilities of those people, and you've set yourself on a mission to say, okay, what do they have in terms of competencies? What can I learn? And where can I get that? The first would be that learning mission.

The second would be to think about the 200 people in that profession, even around that profession, who are the movers and shakers and influencers, who are knowledgeable about that field or that environment or that ecosystem. You want to make it your business to do the deep research, and understand the organizations and individuals who are part of that world, and how is it that you could start to bank on and attend to the serendipity? In other words, try to find circumstances, events where you can lean more about them, and maybe potentially meet them.

The third would be to get yourself in the environment where the exposure to the area that you want to pursue is unavoidable. If you want to do stuff in Hollywood or Bollywood or if you want to do something in London television or New York broadcasting, being in and around those places or having exposure to those places would make a very big difference. If you're an entrepreneur, and you're inventing things in Dublin or Tel Aviv, make sure that you're part of those communities that are doing the stuff that you love, that you're interested in. I think there is associations pretty much for every profession, and you should be a part of it.

It's interesting. Once you start to volunteer a little time in that profession, you might think—gosh, I might not be the most senior person in the room or I might not be the most famous or the most experienced. What's interesting about most professional associations is that they love to have help. Everybody's busy, and you'd be amazed how quickly you can move into leadership roles, or at least roles of influence in professional associations, just because you show up to sincerely engage in helping making events happen, or the meetings happen, or helping their newsletters happen. Think about what professions are serving the areas that you're interested in, and maybe you can't be there physically, or locally because of where you live, start to contribute time, effort, and energy in supporting what those organizations are doing, and volunteering for that, you'll be amazed at how quickly that dimension of engagement will offer you opportunities to meet people who could be co-conspirators, people who would be recruited as partners, people who might become customers and people who might be the mentors that you're looking for, so that you can develop your skills.

That's the final area, which is start to work a plan and find a study buddy, either a mastermind group, or a peer who coaches you. One of those terrifying things we've learned about executive coaching, as an executive coach, is that when we've done global research in major organizations around the world, having a good coach—in terms of having someone who's skilled in your area or understands something about coaching—is certainly very helpful, but the highest correlation of impact on coaching really comes from the fact that you have somebody who's holding you accountable to your goals and objectives. Maybe somebody who knows nothing about coaching or about your field, just because you know he or she is going to call you everyday with ten questions that you wrote, and ask you, are you doing those things today? You can only lie so many times, before you have to say, I'm going to do the crunches, and I'm going to do the cold calls, and I'm going to start doing this stuff.

It is easier to readjust the plan toward a better self than to realize after months of planning, you haven't left the parking lot. It's no good having the engine on if you're going to sit there with it ticking over. Take yourself out of park and click into drive and progress yourself forward!

Which oddly enough is a great segue into our next chapter, progression. We are progressing through this book, half way to a newer, more driven you!

CHAPTER 7

PROGRESSION

I remember feeling this big ball of excitement and nerves as I hung up the phone. I actually danced. It was the start of a new journey. Who knew where this would take us?

I had just gotten off the phone with the lawyer in the United States who was processing my visa application. She confirmed that once the papers were signed and I visited the US embassy, my visa would be approved and we could start booking flights to California. I was beyond excited. My career and my life goals were progressing. I had just married the woman of my dreams, and I felt life couldn't get any better. Now we were about to embark on a new adventure to live and work for Apple in California. I remember thinking, *where do we go from here?* A new job in a new country—it was the start of a new chapter. I was moving forward.

The progression from chief dishwashing officer (A new C level!) to living in California and managing a large sales function for one of the best companies in the world (Apple) seems like a good place to start when talking about progression.

It is a story of which I am immensely proud. Even more so now that I am my own boss and will probably never again work as an "employee" of a large multinational. It's a time I hold dear for all I experienced. The highlight of the first half of my career was becoming the person capable of leading a large sales team and trusted with relocation to beautiful California.

The journey wasn't always easy; there were definitely some setbacks and disappointing days when I thought it would never get better. However, what I always had going for me was my positive belief in my own progression. In my mind, I was headed for a career at the senior level of a great organization.

It was a life goal to live and work in California, and I reached that goal by taking small steps forward, one step at a time. I knew where I wanted to go. I visualized myself working over there, and I powered my vision with leadership, performance, and results. It was an amazing opportunity; and for the three years I lived and worked there, I enjoyed every minute of it.

Fortunately, I had people who believed in my potential. Some of the best bosses I have ever worked for took me under their experienced wings and taught me lessons that would encourage me to keep going. It wasn't all me. My progression was based on the support of my family, my coworkers, my bosses and most of all, my wife. She always believed me in when I didn't believe in myself. Annemarie continues to be my rock and my guide. All of these people deserve some of the credit for my career progression and my progression as a man of accountability and responsibility.

Starting my own business years later was also a progression step, one that defines the second half of my career as an author, motivational speaker, and coach. It was life redefining.

Stepping forward. Sounds positive, doesn't it? As human beings we are always progressing. Yet, some people are afraid of progression. The thought of being successful or pushing themselves onward is foreign to them. I find it's often the fear of what success might mean that keeps them stuck. On the other hand, I know people who are progressing for the wrong reasons. They put progression over everything else and become overly political. They use underhanded tactics to better their own position or deflect away from their own weaknesses by pointing at others around them. Progression is a game for them, it might be not about skill or will, but it is certainly about making sure everyone understands how good they are and how good they would be in a promoted role.

They are also extremely good at sucking up to their more senior executives. Their promotion doesn't come as a surprise, but with a knowing nod among coworkers. Progression here was more about politics and politicking than it was about performance or leadership. I have met many folks like this. Unfortunately, this behavior is expected and rewarded in multinational environments and those people tend to thrive there.

Self-interest and progression are linked closely. We've all seen examples of how "progression" means at *all costs* and I can't emphasize enough how detrimental this can be to the business or work group. Having a plan for progression is important, sure, but so is being present in the here and now and making sure any progress benefits the company as a whole. Healthy progress means pushing ourselves through self-development, planning, and good career conversations but not at the expense of those around you. A good understanding of your own values helps you understand the next correct progression step.

> *To get through the hardest journey, we need to take only one step a time, but we must keep on stepping.*
> —Chinese proverb

> *"The ability to notice the effort in the small steps, reflect on the journey and to keep an eye to the next small step—keep stepping forward."*
> **—Ryan O'Reilly**

Your values are your beacons.

The correct steps forward should have beacons or "lighthouse moments." I call them lighthouse moments, because if you're sailing a ship near land, you need a lighthouse to guide your way safely through storms or dark nights. Without that lighthouse, it's easy to hit the rocks. Your values and ethics are your beacons. They guide you to the next correct progression step. If it doesn't feel right and you're deliberating over the next step, then list your values and what is important to you. Does the next step tick all or any of these points?

When I was debating starting my own business in 2013, I knew my next step was important and needed to be the right one. I was either going to take a leap of faith right then or spend years working up to it all over again. After everything that had happened in that nine months before, it was time for a monumental leap forward. After all, I now had plenty to prove to myself after such a demotivating experience.

Moving forward is about understanding the next step in the overall plan. Just the next step, not the next ten steps. A ship will make small adjustments to keep the progression or trajectory going the correct way. If there are multiple options for the next step, don't worry. Check in with your values and decide which road is for you.

If all the steps are not so clear, and the path seems a little confusing, don't panic! The impacts of the choices you make are important. If confusion has clouded the way, then take time to try and remove the confusion or emotions.

You can achieve this by doing the following exercise:

1. Write down all known choices (number them in order of favorites first).
2. On the next page, do a quick mind map. Write the best word that describes the next move in the center of the page and try and come up with all remaining choices.
3. Review with a friend, colleague, or someone who has your undivided attention and whom you fully trust. (Be careful if this is a person who works with you—you just never know!)
4. Now add any new "good" ideas to the first page.
5. Try and detail the pros and cons of each choice.
6. Make a decision. Make it timely. Don't keep churning over it.
7. If the path is unclear and the decision or next steps seem too large, break them down into smaller chunks.
8. Remember it's a small step forwards but you have to know what your vision of yourself or direction you want to go as base for your decision.

I know another competitive amateur golfer whose goal or vision of himself is to be the best he can be. Any decisions he makes on the golf course around a shot or a competition automatically check with his overall goal. This is how he challenges himself and progresses forward.

LIFE IS NOT PREDICTABLE

If you don't know all the steps or are a little unsure where you are progressing to, just remember this little fact: **life is not predictable**. Once you know and accept this, setbacks become more tolerable in the grand scheme of things.

If you had asked me ten years ago what I wanted in my career I would have said that I wanted to be a great leader and promoted to director at a large multinational by the age of thirty-eight. Very specific, wasn't it? Ten years ago that multinational would have been Apple. Ten years on, I am a director. I am not a director of a large commercial enterprise, but my own company. I never thought my progression would take another direction. It has. The year 2013 was tough progression wise. I felt there was no way forward, when in hindsight it was all building up to one *big* move forward. I am now a business owner—master of my own destiny.

CHANGES IN DIRECTION OR COURSE CORRECTIONS

All good navigators have to course correct. Why should it be different for your own march forward? It's how you handle the course correction that counts.

Take James. He is a successful salesperson who has won awards for his salesmanship and professionalism and finds himself promoted to the job of sales leader over his peers. This is exactly what he wanted. And now that he is there, he feels it is justified. After three months, James is drowning in administration and is frustrated at the fact that some on his sales team aren't getting results faster. His peers all liked him as a sales guy; but now that he's a leader, they feel he isn't the same fun guy anymore and is plenty more serious.

James needs to make a decision. He really wants to be successful at leadership and knows that eventually he will master it. However, he is very unsure of his next step. Does he continue to become a leader and more serious, or does he revert to how they see him and know him—the fun guy. How would you advise James?

Which one of the following should he take as a next step toward being a good leader? Should he:

1. Revert to how people know him, the fun guy good at sales?
2. Charge on as the new leader and start making small changes to his interactions?
3. Find a mentor and seek to improve his current impact and get people performing again?
4. Decide to go back to sales, and maybe try for leadership in the future?

What path did you pick for James? Are there other options?

Like all of us do at certain times, James had to course correct. Maybe he didn't know what the right next step was, but he knew something had to happen. Fortunately for everyone, James sought out a mentor and learned how to get the best out of his team without frustrating them. All while being true to himself as a fun guy who was results driven.

USING DRIVE TO SPEED UP PROGRESSION

As long as you are staying true to yourself and not stepping on the heads of others to progress, then your drive can help you progress faster. Drive is the key factor. How clear are you on where you want to be? What steps will need to be taken to get there?

WHEN DOES PROGRESSION STOP?

Are we always progressing? I believe we are. We should be always trying to better ourselves and move forward. Careers may stagnate, and you might feel like you aren't progressing anymore. Maybe you're not really stuck, but you just need a change of perspective. Progression and self-development are combined forces.

We should always aim to develop ourselves and step forward. Ask yourself these questions:

- Are you progressing in your relationships?
- Are you progressing in your passion? (Have you forgotten your passion?)

- What small steps could you take to make that stagnated or flat-lined career take a leap forward?
- What did you dream of becoming when you were younger?

Maybe it's time for a change in how you see progression, and maybe it means moving in a different direction.

REFLECTION

When we talk progression, it is vital to reflect on the journey so far. What have we liked about it, where is it taking us? Are you on the right path? In 2013, I reflected on how unhappy I had become in my job. I reflected on every positive and negative interaction with co-workers to see where it could take me. In that airport in Brno, reflection on progression got my thinking going. I felt I was capped out, and no further progression was possible. I had low confidence and was not able to see the next move. It was a lighthouse moment.

Have you ever arrived at a crossroads in your life? One that sneaks up on you out of the blue, where you have to make a tough decision on where you're going to go in the future? We can deliberate at these crossroads for a long time—often too long! We weigh up the decision and revise it and shape it and ask friends and seek advice.

George Bernard Shaw said, "Life isn't about finding yourself. Life is about creating yourself."

Are you finding yourself of creating yourself? In my opinion, if you answer this question first then it's easier to decide on that crossroads decision.

CELEBRATION

Plenty of people I coach are ambitious and driven. I coach many entrepreneurs and business leaders. They reach a milestone and dismiss it as only a small part of the overall plan. I am one of these people. I don't celebrate the small successes, instead waiting for the big achievement. However, I am slowly realizing that to celebrate the small wins in life means you are enjoying the here and now. Completing another chapter in writing this book, I started to celebrate. There was no Dom Perignon; it was just an "enjoying the moment" feeling.

When you take the next step and it's worked out well—celebrate! You're one step further along the progression. The milestone will seem all the sweeter when you arrive at your destination.

Tim Cook, CEO of Apple wisely stated, "let your joy be in your journey—not in some distant goal."

You need these small wins to progress to that bigger VISION of yourself. Can you visualize what the next chapter will be about? That's right! Vision!

THE LEADERSHIP SPEAKER AND EXECUTIVE COACH LIBBY GILL

Libby is the former head of communications and public relations for Sony, Universal, and Turner Broadcasting. She's now CEO of Libby Gill and Company (www.libbygill.com), an executive coaching and consulting firm, and is an international speaker and best-selling author. Libby has shared her success with CNN, NPR, *The Today Show*, and in *Businessweek*, *Time*, the *New York Times*, the *Wall Street Journal*, and many more.

While chatting with Libby, I asked her how we change up and create something new and get out of the inertia of the same old boring routine.

Libby was of the opinion that the world isn't set up to help us with changing it up.

Libby: The world's not necessarily set up to give you a hand at that, because certainly in the workplace, what you're good at is where people tend to leave you, as opposed to taking a chance on you doing something new. You did the same. You had a big, successful corporate background and said, "Time to shift gears," as you say, "and do something completely new." It rocks the other people in your life, whether in your professional life or in your own family, when they see you wanting to make this massive change. It causes a lot of discomfort.

They have to be willing to go with you on that journey, or at least to tolerate it, and hope that there's something better on the other end of it. It takes a great leap of faith not just on your part but all the people around you.

Ryan: Absolutely. You need to have that support group behind you, as well, don't you, to help you keep pushing on?

Libby: You do. If you don't have it, you need to create it.

I also asked Libby what advice she would give to someone who was reading (or listening to the podcast) but who was "stuck in neutral" and not progressing forward. She said:

We all know, in a lot of cases, we know what to do. We're just not applying it, because either way we find a lot of excuses. If we didn't, we'd all be a lot richer and a lot thinner. We'd have money socked away in our kids' college plan or our own retirement fund. Figure out where you need to focus. It's not overhauling your life and career in one huge fell swoop. It's saying, "Hey, this is an area of urgency. I'm going to target this first, and I'm going to put some factors in place." One thing that I think is absolutely life changing is having some accountability.

CHAPTER 8

VISION

T he auditorium was packed with 150 people. There was an exciting thump of hearts and electric chatter in the room. The atmosphere was positive and pulsating. The talk was nervous. Something big was going to happen. It was that feeling you might have experienced when you were just about to hear a favorite artist sing live for the first time or witness your sports team live in an important game. Everyone's felt that, right?

Something huge was about to happen.

Most of us knew each other, but this event was breaking down our barriers and everyone was talking to each other. It was exciting. We are all standing in groups, as the nervous noise reached a clatter. Chris went on the stage and found it hard to get us to sit as he spoke through a microphone.

"Everyone, everyone...Hello!...If I could have your attention please!...We are about to welcome our special guest into the auditorium. Can I ask everyone to get seated and ready? We just want to go over a few house rules. This special guest is taking time out of their busy schedules to talk to you today and we want to make sure we represent ourselves right for the duration. No photographs allowed. No questions about Bono. No questions about new products. No questions about his personal life. No questions about profit margins or anything topical that is in the media. Did I mention no photographs? Full attention when our guest is talking. Everything that will be said here today is strictly confidential and you are not to share what is said outside this room. It is extremely important that you listen and ask really good, thoughtful questions. I am sure you are going to enjoy it, as much as I am, but please remember all the don'ts. It is very important. I am going to stay here till we hear he is at the door and then our division head [name omitted] will introduce him to you. Thank you and enjoy it!"

With that, our division head took the stage and said, "it is with immense pleasure and excitement to welcome our next speaker. This person's vision and success is an inspiration to all. I don't think he needs any further introduction. Put your hands together for our inspiring CEO and leader: MR STEVE JOBS!!"

The place erupted. We were all grown men and women, but we shared this star-struck feeling as we all got to our feet to applaud. Steve lightly floated down the steps to the solitary high wooden stool on the stage (another trademark of Jobs). He was relaxed and comfortable in his own skin and by now understood his charisma, power, and impact on people (particularly the employees). Everyone was overwhelmed with excitement.

He took a seat, and smiled and raised a hand. Instant silence. His bespectacled face was bright and smiling. He seemed to be in great form and unstoppable.

The next forty minutes flew by, as Steve Jobs enthralled us with answers to our questions and with his view on the world. He talked about his friend Bono and Project Red, stating that he didn't know how much Apple had paid to the charity, just that Bono had asked him to do it, so he did it. He talked about our products and how far we had come as a company. He gave a vision for the future with great clarity. He knew exactly (or we felt he knew exactly) where he and Apple were going. At times he was witty, and at others serious and everyone hung on his every word. Before he left he said something that amused us all, "Remember that Apple was a company founded by hippies with a vision to create something better."

With that he was gone, and he walked up the steps of the auditorium to another standing ovation. It was a special moment that I bet everyone in the crowd that day remembers. I know it was one of the best days of my Apple career.

"If you are working on something exciting that you really care about, you don't have to be pushed. The vision pulls you."
—Steve Jobs

"The ability to look into the future, paint a picture of what yourself or your company want to become known for. This is your vision!"
—Ryan O'Reilly

VISION

Let me start by asking what you think vision means.

Most people I ask this question don't have an answer. They say it's because they find it hard to think past next month's sales numbers or the end of the quarter or next year. They often say, don't ask us where we are going because we've got too much to figure out first. Small business owners tell me they are concerned with growth, but don't have a vision yet. The ones that really try to answer the question are usually the ones who have the biggest breakthroughs. As Jobs said, the vision pulls you.

Do you actively sit down daily and work toward the vision you have of yourself, your business or your career?

If not daily, do you schedule the activity? Is it part of you? We often hear of business leaders having retreats with their highest leadership/management teams, which sounds great. But what actually happens besides the luxury of the few days away from the office? These are vision sessions. Sure, there might be planning for the upcoming year ahead or tactical conversations, but mostly it's a chance for the leader to create a vision, share the vision, and for the team to help shape it, live it, and start delivering it for the business.

Vision for me is the ability to take time to look into the future, paint a picture of yourself and your business. The painting has to be what will make you happy; it has to be bigger than you'd ever have thought possible. It has to be clear.

Let's review what vision should be:

1. **Big—larger** than anything you've ever done or achieved up to now.
2. **Clear** – simple, accurate, and memorable.
3. **Provocative**— an image that makes you happy!

As Jobs says in the quote above, it has to pull you. It has to be that compelling.

Take time to think about it, what do you want to be known for? What does your business want to be known for? What will your career stand for?

It's important to not get too caught up with the vision of you or your business or your career. You don't want to think about the future constantly. However, it is important to spend time on it and understand that the you of tomorrow will be carved from the you of today and the steps in between you chose to take.

If the vision pulls you and has a strong magnetic draw, then it'll be easy (in hindsight). Vision helps you plot the course. It's the destination. A month ago, I asked one of my coaching clients, Paul, what his vision was of himself. He answered: successful, rich, and happy. I teased it a little more and asked him to write down one sentence that would sum him up in twenty years' time, something that his family, kids or grandkids, his closest friends would all agree on.

Steve Jobs, for example, wanted Apple to put a "ding" in the Universe. What did Paul want to do? My client thought about it. I waited for him to write. Outside looking in, he was already successful. He was a multi-millionaire entrepreneur who was generating speed with his company. I knew his company was just taking on fifty more people, and as his coach I had gotten to know that he was happy most of the time. He was relaxed and always present (one of his many strengths). However, he continued to think deeply about my question.

What was the one sentence that would sum you up in twenty years' time?

It took Paul nearly twenty minutes to get the sentence out. I could see he was really trying to get it right. He hit the nail on the head, just the way he is. At the end of the twenty minutes he turned his page to me to read. He looked up and said, "If I get to that vision of myself, I'll die a happy man!"

He wrote (and gave me permission to print): "He laughed, he loved, he trusted, he was passionate about life, family, and his business."

The point of vision as it relates to drive? As soon as Paul wrote that down and thought about it for a few days, there was an immediate change in all of his relationships. He told me that he had shared with his wife and kids and asked some of his closest friends to always make sure they kept him grounded on his vision of himself. His family loved it, and they wrote sentences for themselves for their own vision of who they wanted to be in twenty years.

A month later, Paul figured out that this sentence has helped him to really want to live up to the vision he has of himself. It's changed his outlook. Rather than getting through the day driving for results and forgetting the important things, he is grounded by his vision. His family and close friends help him keep it real. I am confident this successful entrepreneur will also take his lesson into his business and come up with a big audacious and hairy goal. (BHAG)

WHAT IS A BHAG?

Jim Collins, author of *Good to Great*, says a BHAG is a big, hairy, audacious goal. It's a goal we should all have in life, business, personal, or a career.

What is your big, hairy, audacious goal for yourself?

Your BHAG drives you toward your vision. Dreaming also helps with vision. Some of the greatest leaders and writers had vision. They lived it. They spoke about it and they shared it. Martin Luther King Jr.'s infamous words "I have a dream…"

What's your dream? What do you want for yourself, your family, and your life? What's that vision look like?

In 2013, with my tough work situation, sitting at that airport, I knew my vision of myself had changed dramatically. It was no longer what I wanted, hence all the upheaval that followed and the emotional state at the time. It's important to have a vision, but remember it's not set in stone. Life happens. We change, and what was important to you last year might not match with how you see your vision in the future. It might have to change a little or it might have to be rewritten, but that's okay as long as the vision is congruent with you and your values.

Life changing moments happen when you realize you are not in the place you thought you'd be. They happen when that congruency with yourself is misaligned. Maybe you have money and position, but maybe your values never aligned with your company. Or maybe those seventy-hour weeks are finally taking their toll on your relationships, or your health, or worse, both.

Your vision of yourself needs to be aligned with your values. What are your values? What pillars do you have that are concrete and unshakeable? Usually with clients I draw four pillars on a page. I ask the person I am coaching to write in the four values that are most solid and will never—no matter what happens—be knocked. It's a tough exercise.

Could you do it? What words or traits would you write? What are your core values?

What are your four concrete pillars?

THE VISION CHECKLIST

Keeping yourself on track for your vision.

1. The Vision of yourself has to pull you, drive you, and has to be congruent with your values.
2. Write a vision sentence of yourself and where you want to be in life
3. Check in regularly with your vision and check progress against your vision. Ask, "Is this still the vision I have of myself?"
4. Write your four Concrete Roman Pillars. Check the meaning of each trait and characteristic and be true to those values. Learn the meaning of what it means to be honest, loyal, and trustworthy and live the definition of the words (it's your moral compass).
5. Take time to understand others close to you by asking what their four pillars are in life. You'll be surprised at how pleasant the conversation can be and what is revealed at times!

THE MOTIVATIONAL/INSPIRATIONAL SPEAKER JACK BLACK

Jack Black is the founder and course director of MindStore International (www.mindstore.com).

Hundreds of companies and organizations all around the world have engaged Jack over the last twenty-five years. We're talking nearly half a million people, global participants. I used the opportunity to talk with Jack to get his insight into how we all can really Shift Gears!

Ryan: How much does vision play a part in driven people's success?

Jack: That's interesting. The vision, the power of the vision…there's three things happening. First of all, [there's] the fact that they created the vision. [They] snapped, if you like, the chains of inertia and catapulted them forward. Because they're constantly going back to old habits and then something else happens. They begin to build the momentum because they start to believe that they will. Because they constantly go back to that future, believing that they will, they end up with the thing that pulls them in, as you say. That is expectation. They finally expect it. They just know it's going to happen.

Ryan: Why do some become insanely successful in their fields and others (the majority) don't? What's the difference?

Jack: The great thing about these people, too Ryan, if I can say this, is because they've got so much momentum and they've got so much commitment to their vision of the future, if on their journey they need to change direction, getting back to being stuck in the road, they find that effortless to change direction.

They'll go off in the direction of a completely new goal without feeling somehow that they've let themselves down. They just know a better one will come along, and know, "Let's go after that." With the momentum they can shift. But often, people don't understand this stuff. [They] come up against a block in the road, a tree in the road, or they're stuck in the mud, and they can't for the life of them get themselves beyond that.

They give up. If a door is closing, they just accept that the door has closed. They don't look to see if another door can open. The greats have always been able to find another door. All the great success stories in business are people failing and starting again.

> *"The greats have always been able to find another door."*
> **—Jack Black**

Take the risk and build a vision that will make drive toward your true high potential. Yes, you guessed it we are going to discuss risk in the next chapter.

CHAPTER 9

RISK

Months after that impactful airport meeting with myself, I was sitting at my desk, in the sales division of the large multinational. Things had gotten worse since, and my mood was well below what I had come to expect of myself. Something had to change I told myself, I even wrote it down.

I was standing still. Stuck in neutral.

I tried to coach myself in this instance.

"What would Ryan the coach say?"

I asked myself to write down a list of pros and cons of leaving a high-paying job and good benefits versus staying and sticking it out. The pros of leaving won hands down. So it was decided. I was going to leave the comfort of this particular role and go out on my own and chart my own path. I wanted to be different, and to do that, sometimes we have to stand out from the crowd and stand on our own two feet. We have to take risks.

I've met many high-risk takers, and I've also met and coached risk-averse people.

Generally, these are people who have the vision and the nerve to take the leap. They might fail on their preferred destination from time to time, but they forge on because they believe it will work. High-risk, high-reward people work hard at making it work and then reap the rewards

Has anyone you know taken a big risk recently?

Was it a risk that had everyone saying, "Wow, that's crazy!"

Would you have taken the same risk yourself in the same circumstances?

How did it all pan out?

The greater the risk, the greater the reward.

Risk taking is important when talking about jumping from small steps to big success. Now that is not to say you have to "go big or go home" for every decision you make. However, the most successful, most daring, and most admired people tell us that risk taking and giving "Big" a chance is the only way to leap toward the life you desire.

If you are too comfortable currently and have never taken a risk, that is okay. Many of us are like that. However if you want a better life, want to shift out of neutral, better your career, better your family life and relationships, a risk is what's needed to get there. Risks help us step out from our comfort zones and help us get used to the emotions associated with being a little uncomfortable, and learning while doing so. Look at your vision of yourself now, and in a few years time. To get where you want to go—will there be risk involved?

What are the three biggest risks or barriers to success for you realizing your vision?

List the big three risks:

1. _____

2. _____

3. _____

I usually get clients to start the sentences with "I am most afraid of _____."

Doing this exercise really helps clients understand where they see the risk. Is it the risk of losing face among your family and community? Or do you worry about the risk of losing your savings and failing? Or perhaps you're concerned about the bank loan and how they might lean on you if it doesn't work out.

George Clooney decided to try out for one more part and then pack in acting for good. He was in his mid-thirties and hadn't made a breakthrough. Luckily, he threw all his acting experience into a big audition and landed a part on a pilot called E.R. He obviously didn't look back. That small step allowed him to leap to great success.

Will people laugh at you? You bet. Will some say you are crazy, and it will never work? Sure. There are people in this world who will always find a way to bring you back down to their level. But it's important to realize that they are acting out their own personal fears. Their words have little to do with you and more to do with them. It takes courage to take risks. When you talk to entrepreneurs, they call it bravery. They took and take risks. Remember: the greater the risk, the greater the reward.

Some time after deciding to go out on my own, I found the rewards started to outweigh the risks. I've definitely jumped outside my comfort zone, but have made more connections and had more opportunities open up to me. The initial risk was definitely worth the jump. Starting my own business and meeting many new and exciting like-minded people has opened my eyes to the opportunities that are out there. Taking that risk has given me new energy to race forward. The more I surround myself with other entrepreneurs and people in the coaching community, the less I fear taking risks

"Only those who will risk going too far can possibly find out how far one can go."

—T.S. Eliot

"If you are offered a seat on a rocket ship, don't ask what seat—just get on!"
—Sheryl Sandberg, COO, Facebook

"Take the chance. What is the worst that can happen?"

I am not suggesting that you jump head first into anything that seems to be risky. You'll want to evaluate the risk and have some criteria to help you figure out how much risk is worth taking. Let us first look at some criteria for qualifying "risk" and then look at some tips around making a sound decision that builds your confidence in making these tough risky decisions.

Criteria for Qualifying Risk:
1. Identify any possible risks in the decisions you're considering. List all possible risks. This can take the format of a pros and cons list, or it can be a numbered list 1–10 of how many risks there are in the decision. Think of possible scenarios here like, "We run out of cash flow before sales revenues start coming in." Detail each risk with a paragraph, so that a neutral party looking at the risk would understand it.
2. Reduce the risks or understand which risks can be minimized. Next, go through your list of risks, underlining any that could be eliminated. Are any of the risks that are high cost but low reward? If they are high cost and are necessary to the vision or the project, then go into more detail how much will it cost, what the benefits will be, if there is any way to make it less risky, and what plan b is.
3. Weigh the risks and prioritize. Go through your list and determine what risks fall into the category "low cost, high impact." Any that meet this criteria and look to be the biggest wins are the ones you should chase first. Next, write down which of your risks are "high cost, high impact." Determine what high cost means. Is the whole project/decision resting on this "higher costs, higher impact" factor? If yes, then the risk might be greater than you think. What is required then is a more thorough approach perhaps to this particular risk. Do some more research or consultation with your close circle.
4. Plan. Once you have listed and prioritized all risks, you then need to put a plan behind these risks. In business, this is generally called risk

management or a risk management strategy. It helps to minimize the fear when you brainstorm the potential risks and understand what will happen if they become real.

LEVELS OF ACCEPTABLE RISK

The difference between risk-positive and risk-averse people is the perceived levels of acceptable risk. Generally, an entrepreneurial profile will be extremely risk positive, not caring for the rule book, making decisions more on intuition than on facts. Richard Branson would be one such entrepreneur—particularly the Richard Branson who started out broke and had big ideas. He wanted to create a new rule book, and challenged the "system of the time." These days Richard has many advisors and consultants to help him understand the risks better, but generally has kept that passion for taking risks that others are not prepared to take. A prime example here would be his space program, Virgin Galactic.

Risk-averse people need plenty of planning and detail before they are ready to make a decision. Sometimes this can actually lead to paralysis by analysis. Paralysis by analysis is where there is an overwhelming need for more information and detail to help make a better more informed decision. However, as the need for more information continues, the decision-making suffers. There simply aren't any decisions being made at all. Big business often makes this mistake, particularly when there is a matrix environment and individuals don't want their names on something if it fails. The time has to come when a decision is made one way or the other.

In professional selling, it is this risk averseness or inability to decide that slows down the selling process. Put a cautious buyer or indecisive, risk-averse person in the decision-making process and everything slows down. Statistically it has been proven that the biggest inhibitor to sales being closed is indecision or a "sitting on the fence" attitude from the buyer that prompts no action. As salespeople, we can encourage that decision to be made by creating a sense of urgency around the project. Demonstrate that the risk might be greater if everything is left the same rather than getting the new technology piece or product to make things better.

EVALUATE YOUR RISK TOLERANCE

Write down the length of time it takes to make a decision on what restaurant to go to with your friends? Is it a back and forth conversation that lasts a few minutes or does indecision creep in?

Now pick a really big choice you have to make. For me, it was leaving my corporate management job. What is it for you? Moving city and job, changing career, getting married, starting a new course of study, starting up a new business?

Rate your ability to make this huge decision on a scale of 1–10.

One represents absolutely timely decision making. "I was born to do this and I feel this is the right thing for me!"

Five represents that you need some time to think. "I might seek some outside council from people I trust, but I am definitely going to make a decision that is timely."

Ten represents that you can't make a decision. "I need to talk to more or all people (perhaps even the barista at the local coffee shop). I need to spend lots of time thinking about this and analyzing the information and the opinions of others before I might eventually make up my mind or bury my head in the sand and hope that the decision that I have to make just goes away! (Phew!)"

This rating system tells you whether you are risk averse or risk positive on this particular decision. If you scored yourself 1–4 and don't need "all the information" to make a decision, then you are positive risk taker in this case. Scoring higher on the scale toward 10 means that you are risk-averse and sometimes cannot make a decision in a timely effective manner. Wherever you are on the scale, it will help you understand how you take or don't take risks.

Our attitudes toward risk can uncover why we get stressed making decisions. It can also help point us in our business dealings, is the person we are going into business with or being employed by, limited by risk or risk averse? It's important to understand how that person might make decisions in the future.

"If you ain't making waves, you ain't kicking hard enough" (Unknown)—I really like this quote, and not just because I'm still a fledgling swimmer. It helps us understand the risk versus reward theory. To be aiming and achieving the life we want to lead, we have to take risks—be they calculated or not to get there. We have to make waves, and we have to kick harder.

TYPES OF RISK

At university, I studied and received a B.A. in entrepreneurship. Looking back, it was an amazing course. We were encouraged to look at all the world's movers and shakers in business and not for profit. We had assignments around the key characteristics of entrepreneurs and risk was always present. To this day, I enjoy reading about every type of entrepreneur, and I really believe these people take the biggest risks. However, they mostly take good calculated risks. The "don't bet the farm" or "all your eggs in one basket" is good advice but not always possible.

Which entrepreneurs have you read about recently?

What did you notice about entrepreneurs and the risks they took?

Did you notice that entrepreneurs give up the steady and regular paycheck? Believe me it's not all rosy, and sometimes the risk doesn't pay off. Particularly when you are expecting a different outcome or a faster revenue stream.

Did you also notice when reading about (or being one!) entrepreneurs that they don't work a typical forty-hour work week? They work until the project is finished (which is sometimes detrimental to their health) or until they know they can survive.

A well-documented example of this tenacity is with Facebook's CEO Mark Zuckerberg. Upon securing their first round of funding, Mark could sometimes pull straight shifts through days with his coding team to get something correct.

Let's now look at some of the types of risk we might encounter as we try and shift gears.

Financial

Everyone has financial risk. Buying a new home in a tough market might be an example here, or outlay of huge amounts of capital in a new business before your first sale is made. For multinational business, there is always the risk of currency fluctuations, which could sway your year-on-year sales results negatively or positively. When creating the life you desire and taking small steps to get there, it is sometimes advisable to at least list your financial risks.

Innovation

Innovate or die. For entrepreneurs and businesses you have to keep reinventing and innovating around your product offering. If you don't, someone else will. The risk of staying still can be penalized by being passed over or becoming an "also ran." A lack of innovation in your service or product offering can restrict your business growth and put your business in a place of risk. We see this all the time in the service profession of hotels and restaurants. It's also true for the individual. If we don't continually change and learn and innovate about what value we offer, we can find ourselves getting stale, losing a relationship or a job. Innovation means coming up with new ideas for personal development and growth.

Strategic Risks

Not spotting trends in consumer behavior, being behind the curve in terms of where your industry or sector is going. What poses a threat to you or your business? If you work for a company, what poses a threat to the overall business and how would you plan against this if it were your company? How can you help your business leaders anticipate and plan for these strategic risks?

Personal Risk vs. Public Risk

Is this decision a risk to my health, my community standing, my family, or my career? Is it a risk I am taking personally or will it be well known by others? For example, going back to college and not letting your work colleagues know might be considered a managed personal risk. However, leaving your job and starting your own company might be seen as a more public risk.

FAILURE'S LINK TO RISK

Playwright and poet Samuel Beckett summed it up best when he said, "Ever tried. Ever Failed. No Matter. Try again. Fail again. Fail better."

Western culture teaches us to adopt a winner's mindset and to avoid being a failure. Failure can be embarrassing, and we are taught to fear it. However, when we take risks and fail, we learn. Check out Richard Branson's books on his story. He failed at times and learned from it for the next time. Steve Jobs never graduated. There are hundreds examples of where failure was tough but the risk taking and lessons learned helped those people bounce back to even greater success.

One of the most successful risk takers and businessmen I know is my father-in-law, Tony. Over the years Tony has shared some inspiring stories around risks he took during his extremely successful career as a property developer. In this game, the stakes are high and risks are great. And Tony has always had a fantastic drive to steer through the risks and reach his destination.

One of the earlier risks he took was installing solar panel heating into homes he was building. He was one of the first to adapt this new technology into his business, and it was years before others caught up. Twenty years ago, passive house building was not a hot topic. But he saw the potential and took the risk—and it paid off. Now his houses are in high demand, partly because of the solar heating.

When starting my own business, Tony gave me solid advice. This time it was about the risk. When I voiced my concerns about going out on my own and all that is risked in doing so. His advice was direct, precise, and correct.

"You will *have* to make it work—if it were easy, everyone would be doing it."

Of all the advice Tony has given me over the years, this piece was what drove me to give it a go. I would make it work I thought. I'd have to!

Have you ever seen those ropes that hang from the tree over a summery lake?

Reaching your potential is like standing on that ledge and reaching out for the rope. Miss the rope, and you land in the water. Reach the rope, and you get to swing to and fro into the water. I bet we all remember the first time we tried this. If you haven't ever done it, try to imagine. It's hard to reach for that rope over the water, isn't it?

If you want to reach your potential, you'll reach for that rope. Calculate the risk, recognize it, discuss it, be afraid of it—but grab for it!

THE DIASPORA EXPERT AND CELEBRATED NETWORKER KINGSLEY AIKINS

Kingsley is the founder and CEO of Diaspora Matter (www.diasporamatters.com).

Kingsley and I sat in a café in the early morning drinking coffee looking out over a very beautiful and serene bay in South Dublin, Ireland. It was a bright and early spring morning and listening to Kingsley talk was even more motivating.

I asked him how he approached risk throughout his career.

Kingsley: I suppose I'd use the word "calculated." In other words, I don't think you'd get too far unless you take one risk. So you have to do that and you have to be willing to take it on in all its manifestations. And then, calculated in the sense of trying to figure out best case scenario and worst-case scenario. And try to mitigate the expensive mistakes if possible. At the same time, you realize that there is such a thing as a risk-reward ratio. Unless you're willing to dance with that, you're not really going to succeed. So "calculated" would be the answer. I think it depends on the people. I don't think everybody's cut out for that. I think some people are very risk-averse. Some people like to avoid risk at all occasions. And you have to respect that. So I wouldn't be too prescriptive in it. I would just say it very much depends on the individual. But if you're able to hack-it and if you're able to live with it, then chances of getting greater success will be greater.

Ryan: Fortune favors the brave sort of thing?

Kingsley: A touch of that. You know Wayne Gretzky, the great ice-hockey player once said, "One hundred percent of the shots I don't take, I miss."

Herb Kelleher was the CEO of Southwest Airlines, the airline in the United States and was asked about his marketing plan. He said, "We just do stuff." So unless you're doing stuff, unless you're in motion, unless you're connecting with people, nothing's going to happen. Nothing happens when you're lying in bed at night. So you do have to be in motion. You do have to be active. You have to be out there. You have to be networking is a thing I believe in strongly.

I hope this has given you the confidence to take the risk and keep reading. You can be confident knowing that there are only a few chapters left. Can you guess what the next chapter is about? Yes, you guessed right! Confidence.

CHAPTER 10

CONFIDENCE

T here are moments in life, where 100 percent confidence is required, and anything less is only second best. It requires you to raise your game and it's a winner-take-all type of scenario. That's where I found myself one morning. It was just after dawn, my fleece-lined jacket was zipped up to my chin, and a battered old baseball hat clung to my head.

The waves had a lowly lapping sound as the tide withdrew from the mile long horseshoe beach. The sound was relaxing as I walked along. It was only her majesty, the Atlantic, and me.

The clear blue sky indicated that it was May, but the morning air was chilly and the sand under my feet hadn't heated up yet. Luckily I was wearing sneakers and jeans, and the cold wasn't bothering me too much. In fact there was warmth about me that day—a giddy type of warmth.

My head was suffering slightly from a mild hangover of wine, a late night, and a bottle or two of beer. The previous evening had been a fantastic combination of dinner, laughs, and great company. This was my plan all along:

this beach. Kilkee, Co. Clare had been important for a long time and meant (and still means) plenty to those in the know. The beach, in fact, was the scene for O'Reilly family holidays for years. There was history here. It was a happy history, a family legacy, and a place to comfort you in the difficult times of bereavement. It was special, and it still is.

The town was still asleep. The holidaymakers and residents had not yet risen from slumber on that early Saturday May morning. It was a quiet and connected-with-nature type of moment. For the discerning onlooker this was a scene of madness—one lone man on a beach running in crazy directions with what looked like a brush handle or a long stick. Some early morning street cleaners were out in force emptying trash and chatting with each other. I noticed they were looking down from the high sea wall that broke the border between beach and town.

They looked like they were reading what I was writing and then cheered loudly, waving their arms down at me in a happy fashion. I waved back, slightly embarrassed but still busy writing in the sand. One of them roared "Yahoo! Fair play to you lad!" and off they went on their business.

As I scribbled with my stick on the beach, I saw an elderly lady out walking a dog. She walked across the strand line and I noticed that she was also trying to read what was being written. The lady, with her dog, stopped at the steps, right where the wall broke. I sensed her reading, and I stopped writing and looked up.

She started laughing and waved at me furiously. I had never met her but I waved back and even jumped in the air and clicked my heels a little, like a prizefighter before getting into the ring. She cackled, and I heard her practiced laugh resonate across the beach. She waved and walked on. These two beautiful interactions with strangers still bring a smile to my face to this day, twelve years later.

Finally, I was done. The large writing on the clean fresh sand was complete. The message stretched long across the beach, facing toward the wall with its back to the sea. I stood and surveyed my scrawl with my brush handle supporting my elbow. I couldn't help but smile. My nerves were a little ragged that morning, but my confidence was riding high. It was time to share the message.

Today, there are thousands of social media outlets to publicize. But luckily back in 2003, you could only call or text with phones.

My phone was at my ear and the number I dialed was ringing. The call went to voicemail. I wondered if my plan would fail.

I dialed again. No answer. I tried one more time.

"Hello?" the sleepy voice answered on the phone.

"Hi! Good morning! I am down at the beach for a walk. It's lovely. Do you want to join me?" I said.

"Ah…no…I'm asleep…see you later!" she said before hanging up.

Though the plan seems like it wasn't going to work, I didn't panic. I decided to try one more time and then I would go to plan B.

I dialed again. It rang.

"Hi, will you come on down?" I coaxed nicely. "Just me, you, and the beach!"

"Ugh…Okay…I'll get dressed and see you there in five minutes…but I'm not staying long!"

The five-minute wait turned into ten, which felt about like a month. Eventually I saw her make her way down the strand wall. I watched her walk until she reached the steps. She couldn't read the writing yet. I knew that she wouldn't be able to read without her glasses, so I figured she could only see it when she reached the long steep steps at the sea wall.

So I got into position. I knelt down behind the writing, with the sea at my back. I reached into my pocket and held out an open little box. I was on both knees on the sand with a big broad smile on my face.

After what seemed like forever, she eventually hit the last step and landed on the beach. It was then that the writing became clear to her. She raised her hands to her mouth. I heard her say, "Oh my god!" She stood off in the distance and stared at the writing, crying. This a make it or break it moment!

She started to run toward me. (*Phew*!) Annemarie was now crying, the tears flowing down her face. I took the ring out and placed it on her finger and looked at her from my kneeled position.

Annemarie jumps into my arms and screamed "YES, YES, YES!" at the top of her lungs. I grabbed her and spun her around.

"Wahoo! Congratulations!" roared a street cleaner with gusto.

After a moment, we walked hand in hand away from the beach and the writing.

"WILL YOU MARRY ME?" was scrawled in huge capital letters across the strand, left there for all to see.

Annemarie looked delighted and happy. I was over the moon. I never thought that I would have had the confidence to pull this off. It was the stuff of life dreams, which years ago I never could have foreseen. Her father always says I won the lottery the day I met her and it's true. But that moment required a measure of confidence and strength. It was one of the happiest days of my life and a moment I'll treasure until I die.

"It is not the mountain we conquer but ourselves."
—Sir Edmund Hillary

"The inner belief that conquers those inner doubts."
—Ryan O'Reilly

"Confidence is a habit that can be developed by acting as if you already had the confidence you desire in the first place"
—Brian Tracy

The ability to outwardly exude confidence is critical to success in any field. If you think it, eventually you'll start to believe it. At Harvard, working with campus security, the confidence around the place was buoyant. It was infectious. There was huge belief in the students and people I met. There was belief in their journeys and where they were headed.

There are workplaces where people with huge confidence seemed to accelerate through their careers, but people with low confidence with huge potential remained stagnant. I've seen high performing sales leaders or sales rainmakers with solid confidence and the ability to close a tough deal.

Confidence is not taught in schools. Instead, it's gathered from life experiences from an early age or from a loving family and circle of friends that help you build it block by block. On the sports field, the power of the team's confidence impacts your own. It's a fluid source of inspiration to get stuff done. It ebbs and flows according to the character and the circumstances of the person involved. Like the adrenaline rush of achievement that can result in a boost of confidence, or the oasis in the desert that turns out to be really a watering station for that explorer, confidence keeps us going.

I cannot underestimate confidence's importance to success. You have to believe.

After my terrible and emotional exit from my six-figure salary, my confidence and self-worth were at a record low. The only way to get this back on track was to see a psychotherapist. But even after five eye-opening sessions, my confidence didn't return. For months as a self-employed sales trainer and speaker, it was hard for me to even talk confidently about my services and expertise. I lost plenty of early deals and had to learn the hard way about how important it was to have confidence in myself.

That whole year after starting my own business, I battled with confidence issues and I know it delayed my success. Don't get me wrong. I was in a much better place once I was away from the toxic environment, but it took a full year (or just over) to even start believing again.

As a teenager, I had zero confidence. Taking up rugby was a stepping-stone and getting a part-time job as a dishwasher helped. Having confident friends and watching and learning from confident people helped, too. But confidence in its true form did not arrive until I was in my final year of University. Suddenly, as the year began to close, I realized that I needed to get a job and I had to start believing that I could do it. I had to believe I could get the job I had always wanted, in a fast moving corporation with huge growth potential, and a place where I could soar. I surrounded myself with people who would feed my confidence and help me on the path to achievement.

Confidence really does take time to grow in any particular area. Any driven people I know always exude another level of confidence. Sometimes this confidence borders on arrogance. For me, this is a huge line I try not to cross, but sometimes it happens, both as a colleague and a friend. Once I am aware that I'm overstepping the line, I will try to pull my enthusiasm back. But it's not always easy. I don't believe anyone really wants to sound arrogant or cocky, it's just that confidence spills over at times.

Humility keeps the hubris in check. It's a key skill for leaders, and one that is hardest for many people to adopt. When I coach leaders now, I look for that line and try and understand where the stress points are. Often a client will seem humble or under-confident, but over time they come out of their shells, and when challenged they fight back with extreme arrogance. It's my job as a coach to hold the mirror to this behavior. If this is how I perceive them for an hour a week, how do their staff and management teams perceive them every day?

In the book *Good to Great*, Jim Collins explains that sometimes our perceptions of what a good leader should be are challenged. Many people assume great leaders are those who are extroverted and exude confidence. In fact, great companies and their leaders are different. He says they hold what is called Level 5 Leadership.

"Look in the mirror for failure and look out the window for success," Collins writes. In other words, publicly take the hit for any of your teams failings, and publicly give them all the credit for the wins. This builds confidence in you as a leader.

FAKE IT TILL YOU MAKE IT

Have you ever felt like a fraud in any job you've had? Was the job so important to you that you had to fast-track your knowledge and catch up quick in order to stay?

Did this ever feel like you were the con artist and the one being duped was the employer?

Well if you answered yes to both questions you are the same as me, and the same as the majority of people who find themselves in situations that are outside their comfort zones. The phrase "fake it till you make" rings true and is exactly how confident people will act in a tough situation.

One of my previous bosses once told me his outlook on confidence and on faking it until you make it.

"Ryan, sometimes I haven't an absolute clue what the executives are talking about. I'll be so confused and extremely aware that I can't ask them too many dumb questions for fear they will figure out I don't have a clue. So I just sit back listen intently, rub my chin with my fingers and then say, 'Tell me more.'"

That was his way of dealing with his own confidence and trying to fake it until he understood the issue or concern. It was an eye-opener for me early in my career, and I always appreciated that advice from someone who was my boss's superior at the time. He was just honest. I still meet him regularly to this day for a bite to eat, and he is still enormously honest about everything.

I appreciate the confidence he has, and his candor is a trait I've always tried to adapt as a leader myself. However, sometimes I've overestimated how much I trust someone with personal information. Rather than be 100 percent transparent, make sure you trust the person first.

Too much confidence is possible, if you let it become too important to you. Practicing humility and honesty will make you more real and more of a role model to those in your circles. The barometer should be in the loyalty and interactions you have with people you work with and again if you are true to your vision statement –this will be the litmus test.

HOW DO I INCREASE CONFIDENCE?

Be Dedicated to Becoming More Confident

Next key thing to do is dedicate yourself to becoming more confident (this can be confidence in a skill, or self-confidence). If you persevere and dedicate yourself to acting and feeling more confident, you will become confident. See the quote above from Brian Tracy.

Realize That You Are Worth It

Yes, you are worth it. Worth reaching for your own potential. Self-appreciation and the ability to love yourself as you are (with faults and human) will help you exude more confidence. Give yourself a break from the internal lashings that are unleashed and tell yourself that you are worthy of love and respect.

List Your Strengths

No matter what your critics, your boss, or anyone else says negatively about you or no matter how much they point at your weaknesses, listen, but don't take it too seriously. Know your own strengths. Everyone is good at something, and it's easier for leaders to point to your weakness and faults as it helps them build their power over you. In that toxic job I was in, I realized five months had passed without my boss saying anything positive to me. All he saw were my negatives. One of my colleagues on my coaching course helped me one day by asking me to list my strengths.

My self-esteem and confidence were so low that it was difficult to start the list. Eventually I got there. I realized that I am not perfect, and that I have made mistakes, but that I also have plenty of strengths. This was key in my confidence turnaround. I had over time become my boss's victim, and he knew it. I had just replaced the previous weak one.

Take Pride in Your Strengths and Your Good Qualities

People will like you for that and you will attract similar minded people rather than people that you have to please all the time.

Keep Track of Your Confidence

Bear with me, and let me explain how this will help you increase your confidence. If we check in regularly with ourselves and use a simple 1–10 rating, we can identify where our confidence is at currently. With the hustle and bustle of being connected all the time, working long hours, and family obligations, the stress of the modern work day can creep up on us and eke away at our confidence. A simple rating system, with 1 being the lowest your confidence has even been, to 10 being the highest, what's your level today? Do this regularly in your learning journal. You'll be surprised when you tune into your confidence and self-worth where scale might go. After a few months you'll know and get good at tuning it to it naturally.

Practice Mindfulness

Mindfulness is the art of tuning in. That's my definition of mindfulness, anyway. A simple way to get mindful is to sit in a chair with your feet firmly planted on the ground in a quiet area with no interruptions. Put your hands on your knees and sit in an upright but relaxed position. Close your eyes. Now, wiggle your toes. Put all your attention on them and their wiggling. Notice what it impacts. Maybe your socks? Maybe your shoes? Notice the sensation and how nothing else seems to be in your mind. If we practice mindfulness regularly we will be more aware and it will help our inner confidence in making decisions or

Hire a Coach

I get asked this question all the time. When I coach people sometimes they are looking to be more confident in their decisions or more confident to step out of their comfort zones. Confidence is always a factor once trust in the coaching relationship is established. The coach can be the sounding board or mirror for these tough life choices. So the first thing to increase your confidence is to hire a coach. Professional golfers like Rory McIlroy or Tiger Woods all have three or four coaches, one might be a skills coach, a dietician, a fitness coach, and also a sports psychologist or mind coach. If your back was sore, you'd go see a chiropractor. If you had the flu, you'd go see a doctor. So if there's a block in your thinking, why wouldn't you hire a coach? A professional will hold a mirror up to your issues and areas of distress, indecision, low awareness, or whatever is holding you back. Do your homework and pick someone who comes highly recommended, as every man and his dog claim to be a business coach. Also, choose someone you gel with, because their role is not to judge you, but facilitate your move to the next level.

I am passionate about coaching and making sure the client moves from their current position. I get so much learning and knowledge from coaching that I can confidently say it is what I was made to do. Some were made for farming or project management or starting businesses. For me, I was made to help others reach their full potential. I mark my success based on how much success my clients achieve.

Follow Your Passion. Dream More!

We've talked about passion for what you do. The most confident, self-assured people I know are those who live their passions and dream often. I bask in their confidence aura. Buying a present recently for my wife, I stopped at a small seaside town and went to a crafts shop for inspiration. The woman who owned the shop told me about her shop and her products with such passion that I instantly bought into the place. The customer experience was super.

Dream more!

"How do I do that Ryan? I'm not getting enough sleep as it is."

Here's my answer: you don't have to be asleep to dream. When taking time out to write in your journal, being mindful, and following your passions, spend some extra time to dream. That's what got me started writing this book. In fact, the name of my blog was Part-time Athlete, Full-time Dreamer. I wrote about athletic sporting pursuits and their link to life and dreams. I love dreaming!

Say Hello to Your Insecurities!

Look at what you are insecure about. What makes you feel insecure? Identify it. Hire a coach to help you discover what they are. Ever see a really great comedian heckled live? Apparently, some great comedians (not all) welcome the negative heckler who calls them awful from the safety of the crowd and acknowledge it as true. "Yes, you're right. I am awful I know that; but I'm good at some things," you'll hear them say. Straight away there will be no more heckling.

Be Positive and Bounce Back Quickly from Any Negativity

Speak positively about yourself. Don't apologize all the time. Don't belittle yourself. Take it from me, I used to apologize all the time to anyone, even if I was in the right and they were in the wrong, I even apologized when making a complaint. Speak positively when with friends. Help them believe you are the most positive person they know. Ever been called that? It's been a long time since someone said it to me. I had lost my positivity through promotions and dealing with overbearing dogmatic leaders. Recently, someone commented on how they thought I was a very positive person. It made my week. Getting back to myself is a positive step toward becoming me.

Be positive about life. There is plenty out there to be positive about. When negative self-talk enters your head, picture yourself as a prizefighter and give the negativity a "one-two" punch combination of positivity. Do this every time negativity creeps in.

Accept compliments. Don't shrug them off. Look the person in the eye, smile, and say "thank you," and mean it. I guarantee if you make this change today you'll see an instant reaction and change in the relationships you have. Confidence attracts confidence.

Laugh and Smile

I mentioned the comedy show earlier. Don't wait for professional entertainment to give you a laugh. Create those laughs yourself. Laugh when you hear something funny, and smile at everyone. Honestly, if it doesn't build your confidence it still makes you feel good. If it does build your confidence, notice how many people want to hang around with you. Smile on the phone, smile in person, smile into the mirror. Don't do it if it feels fake, but practice—it is a skill. It is a skill of confident people who are happy or comfortable with themselves. Become that.

LOST CONFIDENCE

"It's gone," one of my closest friends told me. "My confidence, I don't have any, don't know where it went! I'll never get out of this dead end job. I just have to get used to being in this role forever."

This was someone who I have looked up to all my life, and someone whom I'd have never guessed suffered from poor confidence. I decided to listen more. The last few years had taken their toll on him, and he knows now that he will never recover his confidence. It's lost, gone forever. I could relate. But I decided to listen. When did it go I asked him? How bad has it been? How far lower has it go?

"It's at the bottom," he said. It can't get any worse.

Can you relate to my disconsolate friend? I could, more than he knew. I started to tell him that he had plenty of skills and that I could see him get a different job or career by simply tuning into his strengths and building confidence.

"Name five careers I could do," he retorted.

I had no problem quickly listing off a range of careers. At the end of the call, we both agreed it was possible. I talked about the next steps, not telling him what to do, but to firmly try to get him realize that he had a huge amount to offer the world. We came up with a plan and I hoped over the next few weeks and months

I could help him find that confidence again and get his mojo back. I was going to pour myself into this effort because he deserves some confidence and a break.

Over the last few years we've built up an honest relationship. Can you guess what the next chapter is going to discuss? That's right: relationships and their huge significance in everything we've discussed so far. I am confident you'll continue to enjoy the read.

CHAPTER 11

PERSONAL RELATIONSHIPS

aving spent time writing and working on this book, I always knew that toward the end I'd have to talk about relationships. I've been so honest in my failings and my thoughts in the previous chapters. Deciding to be open and sharing some of my personal stories are all to motivate or inspire someone else. At times it has been difficult to write so openly. But again, if I inspire one person to use their drive to maximize their own full potential I'll be happy. I've never said I am perfect and believe me I am not a sage on relationships either. Like you, I've had ups and downs and I continue to learn daily on how to interact better. Hence, this chapter is less advice and more my opinion, as every person is different and relationships are approached and are different for everyone.

When I think of relationships I instantly think of my father and mother. After all, it's this pair that helped me form my own relationships over the years. The man I am today is largely due to their influence and parenting.

First, let me tell you about my mother. What a lady. As a child and in later years, I adored my mother. I have fond memories of growing up, the conversations, the laughter, and the years since. As I said I am not perfect, and being the only son, I am sure I caused my mother heartache and I know I have tested her patience on more than one occasion. She has always been there for our family. A warm dinner and some loving words and gentleness were never far away. I know she worried about me when I was growing up, and all I ever wanted to show her was that I'd be a man she could be proud of. Over the years, I've probably let her down every now and then, particularly after my dad died. We did have some arguments. It was tough for her. I didn't make it any easier. Thinking back, I appreciate her for all she has done for us and am happy for her that she is now getting to enjoy life again.

Having her around to be a grandmother to my children is amazing, I can still see her playfulness come out when she is with them and it gives me nostalgic flashbacks to when I was a kid. It is important to recognize those who are still with us while they are with us, and for me, I try in any way I can to show my mother that I love her for herself and who she is as a person. I'd run through walls for her and I will always be there for my mom no matter what. I hope there is plenty of more laugher to come over the years. Mom, know that you are loved and that my childhood was one of warmth, security, kindness and laughter. Know also that you still mean the world to us all.

Those who really knew my father would agree that he had a special type of charisma. His way wasn't extroverted (but could be at times). His charisma and draw were different. He had a deep sense of caring and kindness and if you made a connection with him it lasted. As a young boy with three sisters, my father was my hero. I remember fondly how deeply and lovingly he would look at us all. I used to watch him even when he wasn't aware. At times throughout my life I saw his eyes dance with delight, at others I saw his eyes filled with tears, and at others he just had a caring look that I am sure most people would remember of their fathers.

Unfortunately, at the age of fifty-four my dad passed away suddenly.

I never got to experience the relationship beyond the age of twenty-four and I often wonder what it would be like to be able to appreciate him and what he did for us as a family as I matured into a man. When he passed, I was moving from that phase of young adult into a responsible man and would give anything to have him around now. I have many happy memories obviously and some memories that raise the hair on the back of my neck, knowing how he stood up for us as a family. He gave up so much for us and never shirked from standing on his principles or stepping in for family. He sacrificed many of his dreams and seemed to spend most of his life working hard to provide. It was always un-wavering support and encouragement. He wasn't perfect but he never pretended to be. As kids growing up, we couldn't have asked for a more caring and fun father. I still laugh when I think of all the games of Monopoly we played for example.

When I think of him now, some years later I think of an encouraging, supportive, fun, honest, caring, gentle and kind man. Little did we know it was our last goodbye just a few short days before he died. He was standing in the sitting room. I was about to head off on a three-hour journey to my new job and it was a big week. Annemarie and I were getting our new apartment together. It was the official start of a new journey, leaving our family for real this time and the beginning of making a family of our own.

As is the case for plenty of sons of that age and their fathers, it was a little awkward between us. I was too full of that young confidence. I didn't pay enough attention to a goodbye that was to be our last, or pay enough attention to him as my dad. I rushed around the house packing, with bags in the hall. It was now time to say adios. It never crossed my mind that the next time I stepped into my parents' house that he wouldn't be there. He had always been there in more ways than one. I had looked up to him and he was just the solid foundation we were all built on.

We looked at each other; there was no laughter, just a small smile between us and some eye contact.

"Well—this is it," I said looking at him.

"It is. Best of luck now," he said back and smiled slightly. There seemed to be a little sadness in his eyes. It was a moment of hesitation between a grown man and his young son.

We shook hands. I had never hugged him as an adult. Rushing out the door to get on my own journey, I was too afraid to show my emotions when that is exactly what I should have done. If only I had the courage to reach out and hug him.

A few mornings later, I was sitting in a sales training class. I had felt horrible all morning. I hadn't slept well. I was feeling off—really off. I just thought it was the end of a long first week in my new job, however at about 11 a.m. someone came into the training room and asked to speak to me. Instantly my father's image came into my head.

Some hours later, as I arrived at the hospital, my granddad Paddy, and my Uncle Terrence were there to meet us as we arrived at the entrance. They stood in the pouring rain. It was like an unspoken guard of honor. My uncle Terrence had lost his brother and looked devastated and my granddad had lost his son-in-law and was full of sadness. I will never forget their kindness in waiting there for me. They hugged me tight and brought me into the family room.

My mother was there with my three sisters. We all hugged and cried. My dad was on a hospital bed. He had a clean white sheet up to his chin. His eyes were closed. His greying curls rested on a small hospital pillow. His skin was pale. My sisters and mother cried. Tears streamed down my face, as they are now as I write. It was just so real and so emotional. It still seems like it was yesterday.

He looked peaceful, but also he looked sad. His expression seemed to be slightly turned down. I kissed him and said my goodbyes. I whispered I loved him and I'd miss him. I hugged my family. The grief was like a vice grip on my heart.

He was gone. He will never be forgotten.

"We can improve our relationships with others by leaps and bounds if we become encouragers instead of critics."

—Joyce Meyer

"Every day I wake up and ask myself how can I drive my personal relationships today."

—Ryan O'Reilly

Using the example of my parents when talking about relationships has hopefully demonstrated how important relationships are to me. Of course my wife and my three young vibrant children could have been the stories to start the chapter. Since my childhood I have relied heavily on other people helping me, guiding me, and supporting me. I still do.

If it wasn't for the people with whom I have the closest relationships with in life during my absolute melt down since that time in the airport, I don't honestly know where I would have ended up. There was compassion from those in the loop. There was patience as I worked through my issues and as I rebuilt my confidence and as my self-worth increased. As sure as night will follow day the bad times will always end. Personal relationships should offer you that room and support to move through your times of difficulty. But you should never forget the effort people put into you at this time. It needs to be repaid as everyone— and I mean everyone—goes through rough times. I bet if you were to look around now and examine your personal relationships you would see someone who is waving their arms for support. They might appear to be good on the outside, but look closer. I now see this, as I had such a hard time personally. So, when I see it I do everything I can to show support to that person. It might be anywhere from something small, or something large, like driving two hours to have a conversation with them.

Essentially it was also relationships that had broken down enough from both sides in my life to have those people at my old job take the stairs rather than get in a lift with me at work. Sure, I had a large part to play in this eventually happening; I was abrasive and called people and double standards out, and was vocal about mediocrity. Looking back I was probably a pain to be around. However, relationships are two sided.

You can blame other people all you want, and I did, until you actually examine yourself and your interactions. Being professionally coached helped me deal with this at the time. I used to sit back and observe how others were interacting while also trying to understand what my facial gestures and body language were giving away. At times I felt so in control of my emotions it unnerved others, at other times, I let myself down and let the stress take hold of me. Hence the nine months of losing power to a boss who thought he never did anything wrong, and if he did think it, his ego could never let him admit it openly.

Some authors and experts out there talk about work and personal relationships being different. I disagree with this because I think every relationship is personal (obviously, there are different degrees of relationships). Every one of your relationships is you with another person. As a sales trainer, any class I teach always hears my opening statement, "People buy from People— sales simply explained."

High performing teams thrive on the personal connections. Just look at some soccer clubs throughout Europe. Their budgets so large, they only buy in the best talent. However at the end of the day the team of eleven has to work together. Sometimes it works and other times they just become a group of people with too much self-interest. Egos grow and get damaged and cliques start. Underperformance follows. Pointing fingers follows. Blame and scapegoating happens after, and then usually the coach gets sacked. Sound familiar in the corporate environment? The real world can be as cutthroat as high stakes sports!

Personal relationships need to be harvested, nurtured, and need to be congruent with how you want to live your life. This goes for your work relationships as well.

Networking is essential for the growth of personal relationships. I love the word connection. In a conversation where you really spend time listening and understanding and relating, you can instantly connect with someone.

Some months back when I was at a conference, I was at a table with people much more successful in business than me and with considerable weight in the business world. That morning before I left the hotel, I pumped myself up. Standing in front of the mirror, I affirmed myself using positive statements and thinking positively. Agreeing with myself that no matter whom I met that day I was going to give it 100 percent in making a connection. My confidence was on the bounce back and I needed this day to be huge from a connection perspective. I wasn't going to be daunted by any conversation or nervous about telling people about my business. I was ready.

I arrived early at the conference and there was one man sitting alone reading and drinking a coffee. Walking straight up to him, I introduced myself and asked could I sit down.

Patrick was a successful entrepreneur; it turned out he was speaking at this particular conference. Immediately, through conversation we made a connection and he became interested in what I worked on. Confidently I informed him I ran my own sales training and coaching business, but had grander ambitions to be a successful motivational and inspirational speaker. There was genuine interest from both parties on the other's business. As more people entered, Patrick said we should swap cards and stay in touch. We have, and since then Patrick has called me regularly to check in and see how the business is going. It might be only a five-minute chat, but we chat nonetheless. This to me is a now a personal relationship. I didn't and haven't asked anything from him. I preferred to build the relationship first. I look forward to learning from Patrick over the coming years and seeing what opportunities open up.

That day I made many other connections, not on the scale of mine with Patrick, but connections that I will hope will grow with time.

At the start of the book, I talk about the meal with Myles. Myles is a fantastic coach, but most of all a super individual. I enjoy his company, as the conversation is always insightful and interesting and he's also a funny guy. His advice that night sparked me into action around writing this book. "Trust yourself," he said. Great advice and so simple, but if the personal relationship wasn't there I don't think Myles would ever have been able to say that so convincingly. It was among the best advice I had received. (Thanks again Myles!)

So what's the connection with personal relationships and drive? It is from these personal relationships that you get the pearls of wisdom. When my father dropped me off at school for my final exams in secondary school he repeated what he always said to me which was, "Just do your best!" The encouragement from Myles and my father stayed on my mind over the years and months since and has helped me become more focused on harnessing my drive. Everyone needs supporters in life.

My drive is *for* my personal relationships. Like my father I have an overwhelming desire to provide. My children and the responsibility of helping them grow into the people they can be have made me more driven. I am also not going to be here forever and my drive is helping me maximize the relationships of those close to me. As a good friend of mine always says, "We are not here for a long time but a good one."

I want to use my drive to better all of my relationships. I want to be driven to become the best man I can be. I want to be driven to live up to my power statement of how people will remember me. Having an impact on and helping people achieve their potential is my biggest driver.

For my family, that's ensuring that I help not just my kids grow but anyone who is in that family circle. The bond I had with my parents as a young man helps me believe that I can create that strong bond too with people I care about and love.

I regularly ask my children the question that all kids of a young age get asked since dawn began. "What do you want to be when you grow up?"

Some of the answers I've gotten over the years: rocket Scientist, Batman (if not Batman, then Robin), a ballerina, an astro-cartographer (yes he was six when he threw that one out!), a teacher, a mom, a fireman, and most recently a Ferrari driver, an actress, and Superman. (My daughter is six and my boys are eight and three at the time of writing this!)

I just sit back and listen to these answers, I always say to them afterwards, "I think you will make a super...(Batman, etc.)"

A dream I have regularly is of when I am older. It's a very happy family home and my kids are all grown up. I dream that they will want to be there and sit with me and my wife and tell us about their dreams and fears and have such a deep relationship that they can talk to us about anything. I don't dream about what they will be, I just want them to be happy and they have become what *they* want to be in life.

Personal relationships are that important to me that I spend time trying to connect with people regularly.

LARGE CORPORATIONS AND PERSONAL RELATIONSHIPS

"You want an environment without politics? – Then leave and go to another small business with a few people. You'll never escape politics of any form in a large corporate organization – it's part of the package. Get good at it or fail. Accept it and play it or perish."

A senior executive (and my personal mentor) sat calmly and told me nicely that this environment I was working in was cutthroat. This was his answer to my statement that I hated the small-minded politics that went on at times in the business.

"Less focus on the customer and more focus and time and effort spent on manipulation and one-up-man ship," I had said

Of course, this guy wasn't a senior executive in a large multi billion-dollar enterprise for nothing. He was sharp and on the money, and his advice was too.

I could have counted at the time how many excellent executives or leaders I had seen fall by the wayside. Not because they were poor at their jobs or bad leaders, but because they lost the political war. I also saw people who ruled by fear, managed up with a brown nose, and people who had their own personal agendas and would then get promoted. I saw incompetence at all levels and I saw brilliance—rarely from the same person. If large corporations had to disclose their employee attrition numbers to Wall Street every year, and it was an indicator of how they run their business, investors would get a shock. Natural attrition is one thing—people leave for better opportunities, or move where they live, or go back to further education. However, attrition in large enterprises is shockingly high in some businesses. I talk particularly about the cutthroat-do-or-die world of sales. There is a 20–40 percent annual turnover and recruitment companies build their own success on this large slide of people. Fees are charged for replacement hires, months are spent interviewing, inducting and training. Corporations spend millions every year trying to get this right.

I help corporate customers understand how they can cut their attrition rates by looking under the hood. It always—more often than not—comes down to personal relationships and culture.

Another one of my senior leaders once told me: **"People don't leave a business, they leave their bosses or their leaders."**

Two months later I put in my resignation and started a new job. He was right and I had looked at everyone that had left who had reported to that guy. There were hundreds of causalities. Some of these people had crossed him or made him feel threatened and paid the price. They were disowned and thrown to the scrapheap. Don't get me wrong, he was also super at what he did and at times his leadership was immense, but his own insecurities got in the way and it was obvious he was out to survive no matter what. He still works for that particular company.

At one stage in this business unit there had been six—yes six!—new leaders in a two-year period. Of course that had an impact on the lower ranked personnel.

SMALL BUSINESS AND PERSONAL RELATIONSHIPS

The executive with his advice to get a job in a smaller company was incorrect in one small detail. Politics and all, its finery go hand in hand in family businesses. Small businesses often have as much politics as corporate entities.

In fact, the reason why many family businesses stall is that there is so much drama in the boardroom and more back stabbing than an episode of Dallas, that the results stall and revenues plateau. Personal relationships are so important in any size of business.

Relationships with your customers are also an indicator of your relationships with your staff and your ability to keep them interested and motivated enough to stay. Besides looking under the hood to see how a business unit is working, I'll also look at the dynamic of the leadership team and their attitude and focus on the customer.

Personal relationships and their importance were highlighted for me in my first year of business. Nobody survives without help and advice. I had to quickly make and cultivate solid relationships with solid people who could provide me with good guidance. I needed an accountant, I needed a website guru, a copywriter and all sorts of professional advice and help to help me down the runway to launch and keep the business going. I still do. In writing this book, I sought a writing coach, a super addition to this process that simply without her I wouldn't have got to the point where you had this book in your hands.

Going from a large multinational to being a one-man band (for the moment!) was a shock to the system. I now have to do everything for my business and can't survive without building deeper personal relationships.

Great minds think alike, but only the foolish think the same.

That's how the full saying goes. With personal relationships it's not good enough to agree with everything. There needs to be a challenge in there. That's how we grow. Personal relationships that can stretch you and challenge you are going to kick you further than having people who just agree with you all the time. However, it's how you react to this is the real story. It's real challenges that will help you drive on or get unstuck from that dreaded neutral position.

People often love doling out free and sometimes-unwanted advice. Sometimes this can be critical and hurtful. However if you surround yourself with people who understand your goals, drive, and ambitions and want to support you, you'll find a different level of challenge. A really good coach can do this for you, sometimes with the neutrality that is needed.

Even if the personal relationships you have are with people with different drives, it all helps as long as it's not their agenda that is getting sent up the flagpole. Sentences that start with "You need…" irk me now. Too many years I listened to people who said "You need…" which really means, "What I want you to do is…"

These are controlling statements from the beginning. Statements shouldn't be demanding; they should be collaborative. It's good to have a difference of opinion and if you trust the person, it's easier to help develop that relationship and move on.

Dealing with conflicting drives and attitudes is important for you. It can give you another perspective or help as a clue to understand what role you want this person to play in your life.

FRIENDSHIPS

There are many kinds of friends in life. Good friends, best friends, old friends, new friends, etc. We classify our friends all the time, don't we? Think about when we introduce a friend to someone: "This is my good friend Sarah," or "Meet my best friend Aidan."

Personal relationships with friends are hugely important. Friends are that connection with people who share the same passions as you, or share part of your past. All friends are important. I have a very simple view on friends and this is how I have tried to be with my friends. Here are some of the rules I live by—

1. **Never let them down.** If you do, be quick to recognize, apologize for it, and learn from it. If they are a true friend, they will understand the first time but might not be so lenient the next time. If you value their friendship you will always be there for them no matter what.

2. **Always be honest with them.** If you can't be honest about love, life, dreams, ambitions, hurt, or happiness with your friends then how will you grow emotionally? I am not suggesting you bare your soul to all of your friends but talk to them with the aim of being open and being yourself. It will surprise you sometimes what the reaction or advice can be or how the relationship can deepen.

3. **Be their biggest supporter.** Don't be jealous of their success. Live it with them. Celebrate and encourage their achievements and their potential. Even if it seems that they are eternally stuck, one day they will repay your belief in them.

4. **Appreciate their difference of opinion or difference in ambition.** True friends appreciate that you are different from them. They don't hone in on your weaknesses and put you down. Again, if they are your biggest supporter they'll want you to be successful. Antagonizing and critical friends who tease you in group settings but act differently in private are manipulative.

5. **Stay in touch with them.** Whatever kind of friend they are, it's important to stay in touch. Make an effort and try to meet them in social situations as much as possible. Catch up. Don't let it go years without at least reaching out for a chat.

6. **Don't betray the friendship or the trust.** The worst thing you can ever to do to a friend is betray their trust in you. Don't even test this. Be true to yourself and if they are really friends, you will do whatever it takes

to ensure the trust is never broken. If it has been broken, you will do whatever it takes to get it back. But do it, don't just say it.

7. **Laugh often and always make friends.** Life is short enough, if we all have the philosophy to make friends and see the funnier side of life wouldn't it be fun?

8. **Understand that sometimes friendships end.** Sometimes you need to make a decision not to be friends anymore. This doesn't mean you cull everyone who annoys you, but it does mean that if you've grown apart, it's uncomfortable being around this person, or if you feel you've done all you can. Make the decision to end the friendship. This doesn't have to be dramatic; it can be just a pulling back from the friendship. However, decide who is worth the effort and who is not. This life is a short one. Surround yourself with people who live and breathe items 1–7 and you'll never have the need to cut ties. Personally, I never want anyone calling me their "friend" if they feel it's okay to continually abuse or take advantage of the friendship, or manipulate situations to make them look better. There are enough of these personalities in the corporate world and I've had my fair share of having to put up with them.

9. **Be Present.** Enjoy your friends company, enjoy their friends, and enjoy their families. This is what life is all about.

In the next chapter, we will talk about leadership. So much about leadership has to do with personal relationships. Allow me to lead you to turn the page to our penultimate chapter on Leadership.

Relationships also mean networking. Do you currently network to advance your relationships and show how driven you are to succeed. I had the pleasure of sitting front row at a motivational conference recently where Keith Ferrazzi, author of *Never Eat Alone* and *Who's Got Your Back*, spoke.

If you've ever seen Keith speak live, you know that he brings realness and uniqueness to spur one to action. He advised to identify three people who could help you achieve your goal and then set out a relationship action plan for how you can get these three important people to help you.

CHAPTER 12

LEADERSHIP

The audience was awestruck with the speaker. Everyone's eyes followed his every move and such was his charisma that he was aware that the slightest hand gesture could emphasize his points even more. His title was not yet CEO, however his executive presence, charm, and focus marked him out instantly as someone who would one day be in hundreds of other companies.

His casual attire of jeans and denim shirt disarmed us and betrayed the sharpness of the mind and the level of executive he exuded. His southern drawl was intoxicating for lilt and engaging for its authenticity. Here was a man who was very aware of who he was, where he came from and what he stood for. Also a man who knew exactly where he was going and how he was going to get there.

It was mid-2008 and the biggest headlines of the day were the financial troubles and bubbles of Fannie Mae and Freddie Mac. This was a nervous time globally, as spectators, analysts, experts, and journalists were all discussing a massive possibility of a huge recession. Some were scaremongering; others were proven correct for their forecasts later. The biggest economic crisis since the 1920s, (bigger than even the dot-com capitulation of the early 2000s) was about to be released to the world. Crash 1.0 would unreel itself into many new versions and updates and scandals the world over. The European Central bank would end up saving countries like Ireland, Italy, Spain, Portugal, and Greece. Austerity was just around the corner for everyone.

The recession's pre-launch had gathered momentum and entire press columns and editorial pages were dedicated to what happened, what was going to happen, and the impact for the world's economies. Unemployment highs were imminent on the horizon.

The in command executive with the title chief operations officer stood in front of the same crowd the CEO stood earlier. After the rock star Steve Jobs left the auditorium and after a short break, the audience was treated to Mr. Tim Cook. Cook had been an Apple executive since the early days of Apple's resurgence with a proven record on outstanding operational ability that had seen the company fight back to being one of the biggest and most profitable in the world. In 2008, it had been seven short years since the iPod had launched "One thousand songs in your pocket," and the company was on an upward trajectory that was unmatched by any other company and would be the basis for many case studies or University education for decades to come.

Tim lived and breathed the brand as much as anyone on the executive or board level ranks. He was also revered. I noticed it as his team sat front row. There was huge respect for his achievements, his vision, his authenticity, his strategic thinking, and his strength of purpose and indomitable will. You could tell they not only like working for him, but prided themselves on it. In my opinion, a true mark of a leader. Externally people thought Jobs was the only one running the company, internally we knew Steve had power and was deeply involved in product design with Jonny Ive and the commercials but it was Tim driving the operations and the business side—the numbers, the sales, and the strategy for growth.

Tim was talking about the iPhone. He was taking us through the performance, by market, the market share, the geographical spread, the numbers of users, the sales totals, and the next steps. The presentation was extremely motivating. This new product had outperformed, out sold, out marketed, and out trumped in every sector and had shaken the industry. Tim held one aloft.

"This is a great, great product. But it is also the cheapest flyer Apple will ever produce," he said smiling.

The crowd smiled back with slight bemusement. Everyone was thinking this phone was the most expensive phone ever produced. The phone cost over $450 with a plan, nearly $600 without one. Media worldwide had bemoaned its perceived high price from the start. He continued.

"More people will buy this phone than any other phone in history and the more people who buy it, the more they will want to use our other products, not just use them, but love them. This device will introduce them to our brand and start the love affair and affinity with our other great products like the iPod, the Macbook Air, and our eco system. Plus all the publicity this has generated for free for Apple will only continue. All around the world, people have been queuing over night just to buy this product, this phone is a *phenomenon* and that is why it is our cheapest promotional flyer that Apple will ever produce," he said. The word *phenomenon* was extenuated and extended for impact.

He delivered his points with precision, his eyes making contact with people in the crowd. The authority and tone of his voice increased his value every second. Everyone still sat enthralled.

He moved on and changed slides. His slides had minimum information. Tim was telling a story. He didn't need the keynote slide to be packed with detail. He knew, lived and breathed the story. The slide was a picture of a mountain.

"Over the coming weeks, months, and even now in the media, on TV and in the newspapers, there is and will be talk of economics. There will be more failure of big names, banks, and corporations, more news about downturns and recessions and maybe even depression. However, at Apple we are, as always, never going to let our success get to our head. We will never rest on our laurels as this breathes complacency. Now is not the time to be complacent. We need to keep striving for excellence in everything we do. It will be easy to listen to all of this hype in whatever market you work in and point at the economic slow down as to the reason we can't grow better, faster, and greater than anyone out there. However, I am going to give you vital advice on what to do with all of this information and how this advice will help you focus on our aggressive growth strategies and how we will, as a team, come out the other side of this economic turmoil as the winner—not the loser."

Tim looked more serious now. A thought crossed my mind on how tough it must be to report to him. Inspiring, but I figured he didn't keep around any fools. He was addressing sales leaders and managers from across the globe whose key responsibility is the delivery of hundreds of millions of dollars for just this particular division.

"This advice, I want you to take back to your teams, write it down and remember it. There will be many companies that won't heed this advice and will then excuse their performances or lose their companies, or suffer large losses or be wiped out. So here are the two words."

The slide changed from the picture of a mountain to a black *keynote* slide that had two words in white block capitals on it. The slide transitioned. The audience read and I could see people grimace. But as sales leaders, we all started smiling—eventually.

The slide read, "IGNORE IT."

Tim smiled.

"I want you to ignore it and I want this to be a period of huge growth for us as a company. No matter what is said in the media, Wall Street, or any other outlet, we have hired and assembled a team of "A" players and this room is the cream at the top. We can and will figure it out and we *will* grow and beat our expectations. So IGNORE IT," Tim said.

His words were delivered in a southern drawl and emphasized in a tone for us to feel the gravity of his words. We did. After his speech, not one person in my group could get over how inspiring a message it was. We weren't surprised by Tim, but definitely more in tune to him as a leader and were ready to answer the battle cry for growth. It was extremely motivating to listen to. I watched the other senior executives reactions. No one squirmed. They knew this was coming. In fact, they all nodded in agreement.

Years later, after I left Apple and followed the story, like everyone else on the planet, I used to be surprised when commentators and reporters would question if Apple would survive without Steve Jobs and whether Tim was the man to lead them out or not. Usually I'd be stunned by what some writers presumed they knew about the new CEO, Tim Cook. Perhaps his private and out of the spotlight personality up to then had not added to their confidence. Perhaps the fact that he had—with his team—turned around the operations of a company about to go bust as recent as 2001 was missing from their research. The media seemed like they knew nothing of his pedigree. But I (with hundreds of others at Apple) knew how valuable he was to the company. Tim is a stellar leader and someone whom I'd travel across the world to hear speak again, not to mention an opportunity to ever work with him.

Tim was "drive" personified. The company, the executive team, the sales leaders, the division heads were all the most driven individuals I have ever had the courtesy to work with. I always knew I was "driven" but when I worked at Apple I never told anyone that I was because there were hundreds of people that I would rate as very seriously driven people. It is no wonder that Apple has this huge success nearly spanning a decade, record profits, and record sales year after year. Of course the products are out of this world, but in my opinion so are the executive team and the focus for results and the drive to be better at this company.

Desperate times can make or break a company. Apple never forgot how close they had become to being dissolved. That dark side was now engrained in the psyche of all those who run the business; it's what kept their hunger sharp and thirst for more unquenchable. Leadership was rife.

"If your actions inspire others to dream more, learn more, do more and become more, you are a leader."
—John Quincy Adams

Leaders charge and forge ahead, sometimes on their own, until one day they look behind to see a crowd wanting to support and learn from them.

I am a student of leadership. I always have been. Information about world leaders, sporting icons, inventors and business titans is the knowledge I craved and still crave as I get older. I have had the privilege of being led by some great leaders and of being in the company of other great leaders. I also have had the experience of working for leaders who lacked passion, leaders who weren't good leaders, and leaders who would rather use their own agendas to get themselves ahead or out of trouble. At times some who called themselves a leader, maybe leaders in title but do very little "leading." Leaders of deflection are what I call them.

It's safe to say as I review the list, that all of them helped me understand the do's the don'ts of leadership.

When I coach people in leadership positions, I ask them what kind of leader they think they are? What kind of leader do they want to be? At conferences or meetings I've always taken notes on the nuances of the leaders on stage— their presence, their impact, and their drive. I even carry a specific moleskin notebook with me to take notes on how they lead. I can spot the frauds or great pretenders a mile away. When I meet a leader I know it and I always try and learn more from them. Leadership tips can be found everywhere. I've also met leaders who are humble, some who are arrogant, and some who only need to tweak some behaviors to unleash a force of leadership but who can be too blind to their weak spots.

On the sports pages of any newspaper, you will read stories of sacrifice, of humility, and of great deeds under enormous pressure. The papers and sports magazines have great stories of perseverance, adversity, and adjectives to describe the feats of the particular team or individual athletes.

As a marathoner myself, I can appreciate the leadership learning from running 26.2 miles in one go. I've written about this on my blog. In fact, I love the subject of leadership so much, that I am pondering studying for a master's degree in it and perhaps even writing my next book on it someday (after the first one is done of course!)

I envision my learning to continue and I know I will be able to continue to help and impact leaders through my leadership coaching programs and one on one leadership coaching.

As someone who started their leadership journey at the age of twenty-five and led large sales teams in Apple and another large IT multinational. At Apple I was given a team of twenty accomplished salespeople as soon as I joined the company. Most of them were older and more experienced than me and they were a diverse team of language and country.

It was a deep-end learning experience. Apple's growth and some key people helped me mature into a leader. However, I'd be the first to recognize that I didn't know everything. I made a lot of mistakes and was probably the least political leader in any of the teams or businesses I worked with. I was perhaps too direct or too honest at times.

I was interested with a passion in being led by leaders who had my back. I was passionate about leading people who knew I had their back. My leadership passion extended to the customer experience and this was always how I tried to motivate and inspire those who worked for me. Some who I led remain firm friends today, and others still would not remember me too fondly. I am not going to apologize to this second set of people. I'm human. I have my faults and no one more than me is aware of them. However, I always backed and was proud of any team under my remit. But know I did some things well and some things not so well. I learned every step of the way and was always reflective.

Years later it's amazing how many I still stay in contact with, having recruited, trained and led as many as 500-plus salespeople.

So what are the traits or qualities of a great leader?

This is difficult to answer as there are so many and so much thought on this subject. However, I've developed something easy to remember and if you can display these traits or do display them you'll be doing really well.

The statement starts with LEADER. Always remember no matter where you are or what the circumstance the conscious decision can be made to lead. Here's what each letter stands for. How many can you circle?

L: Listen, Learn, Lead, and Loyalty
E: Enthuse, Encourage, Empower, and Engage
A: Authentic, Awareness, and Advancement
D: Develop, Dream, Discuss, and Drive
E: Execution, Leading by Example, and Excellence
R: Recognize, Results, and Reward

1. Listen, Learn, Lead, and Loyalty. One of the most important roles of a leader is to listen. Plenty of leaders I've met don't have the skill to really listen. When we deeply listen we learn. When we learn from listening we can actually call what we do leading. This does not mean you lead by consensus or lead by popular opinion. You learn to listen for learning to lead well. Promote loyalty by being loyal to your team. Tell them you will be loyal and don't let them down. Leaders who build loyalty to a high level are usually leaders who move on quickly. These days loyalties can be fickle in work environments.

2. Enthuse, Encourage, Empower, and Engage. Of the many leaders I have worked with, for, observed, or coached, the ability and skill to enthuse or motivate those following you is as important as your analytical skills or as your political power. AS a leader, if you enthuse those around you about the vision, encourage them to be enthusiastic themselves with their own teams, and encourage their strengths, you will empower those now loyal team members to make decisions that are right for the business. The result is engaged employees and teams. We all know engaged teams are more productive. There is a separate industry on just that employee engagement. High performing, achieving teams don't just happen. Someone in that team needs to be enthusing, encouraging, empowering or being empowered themselves. And as a result, the team members that are 100 percent no-matter-what-shit-hits-the-fan will remain. You, as the leader, need to continue to repeat these four things.

3. Authenticity, Awareness, and Advancement. Books by the dozen are available on authentic leadership and what it means. However, most of what you have read so far should help you understand what authenticity is. Authenticity is being true to yourself but always being fully aware of the impact of being yourself. Being aware or having awareness of how you impact people will help you advance everyone, and the business will advance in great turnover, better productivity, and a better reputation as a destination employer.

4. Develop, Dream, Discuss, and Drive. Develop your team; spend time investing in your most valuable resource. Don't have excuses not to

develop your team, such as time ran out, or there was no budget available, or it wasn't a priority. Make time to develop it. Dream on your team. This might be a funny word to see attached to a leadership quality, but I personally adore the word dream. If it wasn't for leaders who dreamt of a better world, or better products, or better customer experience, the world would be still dull! As a leader, dreaming means vision to me, and it's more than important to you as a leader. People need to know where that vision is pulling them. Discuss the dream. While discussing it you are involving and developing your team. Listen to them. Discuss is also relevant outside your team. Some of the best learning can be harvested through networking. As a leader, don't be insular. Drive your team (I love this one). Drive your team, drive yourself, drive your business, and drive your customer experience. Be driven for results and driven to become a leader worthy of the title.

5. Execution, Leading by Example, and Excellence. No matter whom you are leading, whether it's a sports team, a work group, or a large corporation, if you are leading then usually there will be results of some kind. Execution is the art of getting things done as a leader. Execution gets those on the "team" involved to achieve. Getting things done, or execution, needs to be the example you set as the leader. Every leader can impact their charges positively or negatively. If leaders do the right things like focus on people, motivate, and inspire, they will be promote a positive environment and their leadership will have a positive impact. Einstein is a man worthy of many a good quote. I like this one from him: He said, "Setting an example is not the main means of influencing another, it is the only means." Excellence and dedication to excellence will help raise the bar of standards. Be an excellence leader not just an excellent one!

6. Recognize, Results, and Reward. If you recognize the people you work with and lead, drive them toward results, and reward them with one thing only—loyalty—you will go a long way to being the leader everyone dreams of becoming. Recognition is super important these days to ensure people understand how important they are in the grander

scheme of the business/team. Recognition is a kind word every now and then or wanting to always see the good in people. Letting go of your ego is one of the hardest things to do as a leader. Leaders who are very critical typically have their own self-confidence issues.

That's my list. Of course you could write your own too. Try it —what words would you put in for LEADER and how would you explain it to a new team or your current team or live it as a leader?

For most teams I led, I used to take them through what working for me meant. I would cover the above list in detail and talk about loyalty. Some team members over the years shifted their gears and worked above and beyond and got promoted. Others didn't think it was their remit to go charging ahead. But luckily they were in the minority. I am lucky to be still proud of those who worked for their achievements.

Leaders fuel their own internal drives by achieving results through their team. Exceptional leaders are those who recognize the importance of their team and surround themselves with capable driven people at the highest levels. Their drives are focused solely on helping that unit be successful, to grow, and to be the best team they can be. Where I am from there is a local captain of a professional rugby team and every time he is interviewed, you hear him talk like a leader. He always takes full responsibility for his failings or collectively as a team, however he always also manages to set an extremely high bar for excellence. He seems to strive for it. It's his way of transferring his highly driven personality onto his team. They simply don't want to let him down.

Not a leader currently? That's okay too. If you have ambitions to lead, drive is a perfect way to get you started. Remember to become a leader, first become a student of what a good leader is, what they do, and how they act. Take notes on your current leaders in your work/life. W hat do you notice? Years ago I started taking notes on every senior leader that presented or that were present in the same meetings. When you observe good leadership you may remember it, when you observe outstanding leadership you will never forget it's impact. The notes on these leaders helped me show everyone was real and everyone was learning still. No one even the best leaders, are perfect. But more of that in my next book perhaps!

What would you do different or the same as them? Ask yourself what resonates with you from the leaders in our society. Does this leader have humility or are they ego driven?

The journey to being a leader starts with you stating that as one of your goals. Who are the three people that you need help from to get there? Remember, you also don't have to be paid and have the title of being a leader to be called one.

Being a leader is about taking your role currently and becoming passionate about it and mastering it. You can also lead by example. Leading is about understanding where you want your final destination to be. Do you see yourself as a leader or not? Then, it's about verbalizing it to those people you trust and those who can help get you there.

Show your drive through your results and how you interact. Take extra responsibility and give it your all to build a positive reputation of someone who can get stuff done. Speak with other leaders to understand how their journey started. Some of my coaching clients tell me that they never wanted to be a leader. They just fell into it. Some get frustrated with everything that goes with it. However others really relish the challenge and want to become more impactful, more inspirational, and be able to develop their teams.

My key driver as a leader was always to get my team members promoted and moved on. I was lucky that I had some brilliant leaders see my potential and invest in me. Liking this approach, I decided that was the type of leader I wanted to be. Of course helping focus develop and trying to move their careers on meant delivery of sales numbers first and foremost. If you deliver as a leader, your stock should rise.

I have had the opportunity to work for very driven leaders. However, the ones who were too driven, left a wake of casualties. They drove people too hard and with little or no development which led to burn out or these people leaving.

Leaders can be over driven for results. When results count more than the people do, then there is an issue. When results are delivered and people are engaged and motivated by the journey, they will stay.

Dr. Phillip Matthews on leadership:

You look at all game changers, they are driven. They have that unwavering self-belief, that unwavering focus. I don't think you can change a game unless you have that. I don't think you can change a game unless you are driven. First person to make it to the South Pole or the North Pole, that's drive and unwavering self-belief where the rest of the world thought that's not going to happen.

CHAPTER 13

FULFILLMENT

I t was a dreary afternoon in London. After a rain soaked walk down the shopping streets of Oxford and Regent, I decided to retreat to a local pub and over a coffee start this chapter. I saved the best and greatest topic for last—the area of fulfillment.

As I strolled, I observed people. In moments like these I have a quiet interest in what's going on with everyone who passes me. I noticed not one person was smiling, and some passed by in that phone-led type of walk. You know the ones— heads stuck on their phones, walking with a zombie shuffle, and not paying attention to where they are walking. Obviously this could be New York, or any other city in the world. We are connected, but not connected. Here, but not really here. Pondering what fulfillment means to me, I sat in front of the blank piece of paper and tried to define what it meant for me.

Years ago I'd have had twenty different answers for you on what fulfillment means. Three years ago, I might have come up with ten, but now I struggle to come up with more than three. I was full of ambition and for a while now I have been trying to figure out what I want. Leaving the corporate world and setting up my own coaching, speaking, and training business has been a good goal toward fulfillment for me. However, I haven't been an overnight success. I continue to drive toward the value I know I can add. A runaway success for me is where I am constantly in demand for speaking engagements or to coach people. I am passionate about the coaching relationship and passionate about becoming that professional speaker I always wanted to be.

Fulfillment is the reason why I decided to write a book. I aimed high and I wanted it published by the best in the business. I wanted it to have a chance of being good! But completing it, to be honest, has been fulfilling. When one of your life goals (to write a book) comes about it can seem a little strange. It feels like through this process I have fed my passion for writing. I didn't write it to be a successful author. In fact, I've never allowed myself to believe that I've written a best seller. However, I am tremendously happy that I have fulfilled this life goal of mine.

I am sure as I mature as a writer that I will look back at this as the moment I stepped off the ledge—this leap toward being fulfilled.

I've run and completed a good number of marathons, and I remember this anti-climatic feel to when I ran over the finish line of the first one. It was an awe-inspiring journey along the Big Sur coastline in California. I had spent months training and when the event was over and I crossed the finish line, I became a little despondent coming home in the car. Sometimes we can get so caught up in the final destination that we forget that the journey is a bigger part. It's the day to day that we need to love more. Luckily, that's how I approached the writing of this book. Every time I started writing I asked myself, *am I enjoying this*? If I wasn't enjoying it I'd simply stop and come back to it the next day.

As a parent of three children, my life has become more fulfilled. I now share in their dreams, hopes, and fears much more than I do my own. I want them to be successful, have great childhoods, and to be able to guide them to become the people they want to be. This idea fulfills me. When I left my corporate, high salaried job to charge ahead on my own, I was really on a journey of fulfillment.

The place I was working was no longer meeting my fulfillment needs. My kids knew me but didn't really connect with me. Simply, I was never there. Now I feel it is my main mission to be there for them. They are full of optimism; they believe they can do anything.

They are my kind of crowd and it's a pleasure hanging out with them, talking to them and finally I can say, they know me now. There is a real connection. Often you hear of executives wishing they could get that time back when they weren't around for their kids. I hope I can continue to be around for them, as their happiness is now my fulfillment goal. I imagine a scene in years to come where they all want to be communicating with my wife and me, and want to be in our company with their families. If we achieve that as parents I'll be truly fulfilled as a father.

If my kids know I am there for them, like my parents were there for me or if they grow up to be kind and care for others and chase their dreams this will be my true fulfillment. However, I am trying to learn the lesson of living in the present.

Our eldest Michael just turned eight year old. It's hard to believe but our parents were right. Time sure does fly. Our gorgeous daughter Emma is nearly seven and Liam our last, is nearly four. Seems like yesterday all of them were babies, gurgling and cooing as they ate their food or explored crawling for the first time.

It does go so fast. Not just parenthood, but life. A blink of the eye and I am nearly forty. I bet you can relate to this. Doesn't it seem like yesterday when you were leaving high school or in University? This is even more reason why living in the present requires us to stop, engage, and be in the moment.

If I were to take money and material possessions away from you and give you enough food and water to be healthy and there was a promise of a tough winter ahead, what would you do differently to connect with your circumstances and the people in that moment? Could you survive by canceling the television channels and reading and entertaining more as a family? If I asked you the same question in the summer, it'd be easier right? But the winter, for a lot of us is dark hours and cold houses. In the winter it's often the daily grind and television, right?

At a training course on human analytics recently I was shown a profile of my own personality and traits. The trainer looked at my report and challenged me by and said, "Are high achievers people who will ever be fulfilled?"

It was a great question. I realized that maybe the fulfillment I am chasing is never going to get me there fully. It is going to get me to my goals for sure but I don't think it will land me where I am fulfilled. There will always be a desire for more.

What things could you do now to make your life more fulfilled?

Think about my coaching client, Paul, I talked about earlier. He had money in the bank, a great house, and a thriving and growing business. It wasn't until he wrote down his vision statement of how he wanted to be seen by his family and close friends that he started to feel fulfilled. However, it wasn't going to stop him being a high achiever but it did help him put the people where he received most happiness and potential fulfillment as priority.

> *"I have seen business moguls achieve their ultimate goals but still live in frustration, worry, and fear. What's preventing these successful people for being happy? The answer is they have focused only on achievement and not fulfillment. Extraordinary accomplishment does not guarantee extraordinary joy, happiness, love, and a sense of meaning. These two skill sets feed off each other, and make me believe that success without fulfillment is failure."*
> **—Tony Robbins**

> *"It's not the type of car you drive, the clothes you wear, the house you live in, the money in your bank account, it is love, passion for life, family, laughter and learning that will lead you to true fulfillment."*
> **—Ryan O'Reilly**

Here are my top ten tips on how to become more fulfilled:

1. **Keep it simple—not material.** Too many of us are working hard, earning money, and then buying things we "need" or material goods that make us feel good. Don't get me wrong, I love nothing more than to

treat myself every now and again with some new running or cycling gear or a new electronic gadget. The challenge here is to be more fulfilled. Can we live lives that are more fulfilled by keeping it simple? Of course we can. Our world is a material world and it is difficult to avoid all the consumerism. What habits or passions do you have that don't require material items? If you sign up to the belief that family matters, spend time with them. If you believe mediation and yoga are outlets for keeping your brain clear, then meditate and practice yoga. If we are driven by material possessions and things all of the time, something has to give. We'll end up being less aware of those around us and become selfish. Our affinity to "things" will define us. Keep it simple. Do the things you'd do if money couldn't be spent. Take the dog for a walk, have hot chocolate dates with your kids. There is plenty we can do in this world of "everything, 24/7" to make ours simpler.

2. **Show gratitude whenever you can.** I had forgotten how to show gratitude. As part of my journey I am now making an effort to show thanks to those I love. This isn't about showering presents or gifts. It is about those moments when you can offer a "thank you" or "I really appreciate you" Having tried this for a while, I've seen a huge strengthening of my relationships. Even if it goes unnoticed, by theory it will all add up over time. Say thanks. Don't wait until later!

3. **See the good side of people. Believe in others.** I believe in everyone. Everyone has a story to tell and no one person is better. In western society these days, we make plenty of assumptions about others and our opportunity to judge sometimes clouds our ability to appreciate and see the good side of folks. Who in the world sees you as their biggest cheerleader? Who do you know who is down on their luck and has made mistakes, and what could you do to help them feel believed in again? It doesn't have to be financial, just a kind word. Has this ever worked for you? Another way to achieve this is to avoid malicious gossip and rumors.

4. **Forgive others and move on.** We all get hurt, don't we? Co-workers, bosses, peers, friends, and family—anyone can hurt you and it can

sting. Whether it's unmerited criticism, anger, or hurt, it happens. I've personally found that as soon as I forgave those who upset me (particularly those in my last corporate job) it helped get over the pain. Rather than whirr it around in my head and become introspective and burdened by their issues, I forgave and let go. Forgiving is a good form of fulfillment. By the way, forgiving doesn't mean memory loss! It is good for you to forgive. It does not mean you forget! Oprah Winfrey once asked Deepak Chopra, "Who would you like to forgive?" He answered, "They are already forgiven."

5. **Forgive yourself and move on.** We are our own harshest critics. For years my inner voice would do a better job of being critical than any nasty boss, co-worker, or political mover. Their words at times just compounded my inner voice. This is why I started running. To make that inner critic tired I started listening to positive motivation. I've found Glenn Harold extremely good at helping me silence my inner critic. Once you can learn to silence it and forgive yourself, you'll be far along the path of forgiving yourself also. The inner critic, if not silenced can lead you down a path of low confidence and even depression. Learn to spend time on your own and practice mindfulness when you're inner critic makes an appearance.

6. **Don't forget to laugh and make others laugh.** I am the world's worst comedian. In fact I am so bad at telling jokes, I try and avoid it in business situations. If I really trust the people that I am with, I'll have no problem trying to make them laugh and laughing at myself in the process. Friends and family of mine will all agree, if I find something funny, I keep going until it's not (it can be rather annoying). There are many serious people in the world, and there is a time and a place for comedy or fun, but if we make it part of who we are as individuals it can make the day pass and make us feel good. At home, with young kids, I am not afraid to be goofy and make a fool of myself. If my kids can enjoy that and have fun, then years from now they will see laughter in many tough situations. My father and his brothers and sisters took each other less seriously and it always led to hilarious stories and plenty of laughter.

7. **Stop Listening to your inner critic.** That voice. The negative side. The devil sitting up on your shoulder whispering things that stop you doing and taking action. Tim Gallwey's book *The Inner Game of Work* is a great read. Gallwey helps you understand how to manage your inner voice. Silencing it can help you live the life you want and letting it win means you will want to achieve loads, but the only person stopping you is yourself. Say "quiet" to that inner voice and go chase your dreams!

8. **Welcome adversity and challenges as a way to grow.** Open the door to adversity and challenges and throw them a welcome party. As long as we live our lives happy and with the knowledge that adversity will happen, we will be challenged. Then, it's easier to recognize it and use it to grow as a person. Ever heard the term character building? Look at every obstacle that has that extra addition, if conquered, to help you become a better person and someone who will help others. Cycling the length of Scotland and England recently on my bike thirteen hours a day in adverse weather conditions had me smiling from time to time. After the physical pain subsided or was numbed I'd allow myself every hour or so a wry smile at how much the challenge was throwing at me mentally. I knew with every pedal stroke my tenacity was getting more finely tuned.

9. **Read books that are good for the soul. Enjoy nature. Pray.** If you read books, which I know you do as you are reading this one, pick up a book every now and again that will make you enlightened, positive, and focused. Read your book in a park, a forest, or on a beach with the waves washing over the shore. I guarantee you a good for the soul read will be a positive benefit to being fulfilled. I put the word pray here also because spirituality is becoming more and more important no matter what you may believe or whom you may worship. Use prayer to be thankful and to send good thoughts to those in need. For years I never prayed. Since my father died so young, I found it hard to have faith. A good friend told me recently that he reclaimed his faith and it has made all the difference to his life. He prays often now and you can sense this

calm in him. One day on my long solo cycle I started praying, it made me feel more connected.

10. **Travel off the beaten track and slow down.** Walk to work a different way. Go to a country in the world that has always appealed to you, but go seek the locals, not the tourist traps. Pick up your bike and cycle for a few days with only panniers full of clothes and the open road as your agenda. Slow down and be present in these moments. Years ago, I was at a temple in Bali, Indonesia. There was a monk there who was so deliberate in how he walked, talked, and even breathed. He was fascinating to watch and I remember being in awe of his own personal happiness. Speaking with him gave me an enormous sense of his presence, he was present in every moment. Seeking out new friends and new cultures and learning a new perspective on life can help you appreciate what you have already.

My hope for you, as you move onto the next phase of your life is simply that you become fulfilled or experience fulfillment. That is what it's all for. The long hours, the sacrifices at home, the emails, the phone calls. It is all about eventually being fulfilled. If we make a conscious effort to do the above ten things in our lives daily and if we agree our drive and our potential can deliver, fulfillment will be in our lives. My hopes for you are the same as they were when you started reading. I want you to live up to your own potential. Use your drives and motivations to master your area of expertise and to nail down what you want from this life of yours.

Experience fulfillment today. What time is it now? Anyone awake in your house? Is it morning time and you are on your own? Are you commuting on a train?

It doesn't matter what time of the day, just pick up the phone or talk to those who are dear to you. Tell them you appreciate everything they do. Make them laugh. Smile with them. Turn off the television and talk about your dreams. Ask your kids their dreams. Tell them yours. Excite them with the passion for life and passion for people. Make that your legacy. Be there for someone you know who is having a tougher time than the rest of us. Reach out.

Running marathons have taught me two things.

1. Enjoy it now while you can. One day you won't be able to run.
2. It's not about the finish line, it is all about everything that happens before it!

My dreams are full and plentiful. There will be failure along the way and probably disappointment. I am ready though. I will embrace challenge and balance it with my drive to be the best I can be. Eleven time Olympic medal winner, swimmer Matt Biondi said it best "Persistence can change failure into extraordinary achievement."

I asked every person I interviewed for this book: What does fulfillment mean to you? Here are some of the answers:

The NFL Quarterback Mike Kafka:

I think as long as I can look at myself at the end of the day and feel good about what I'm doing. I do realize I am a lucky person. I have a great wife, a great support system, great friends and family. Business and football aside, that's the most important thing to me is my friends and family. And I think at the end of the day, as long as they're happy, I'll be happy.

The inspirational speaker Jack Black:

For me, fulfillment is where you're striving in your own way to have the wheel of life in balance. You're doing the best you can with the resources you've got to see if you can keep it out to what is at perfect balance. That for me is fulfillment.

Family man, Iron-Man, endurance athlete, and senior human resources executive Stefan Trappitsch:

Fulfillment to me personally...Is not related to money and is not related to wealth it's just totally different. Fulfillment to me is having a great family, and keeping the family together. That is fulfillment to me in my private life. It's so hard, particularly to balance between the sport and business, and starting a family as well, friends and all that. To keep the inner circle close and connected it's hard work but it's worth it.

The diaspora expert and successful networker Kingsley Aikins:

I think it's having a sense of having given something your best shot and not always succeeded, not always won. For every winner there [are] going to be losers. Trying to lead your life as best you can give in the constraints on a moral and ethical basis is probably a good sort of definition of satisfaction and success. It might be something you never get to. Fulfillment might just be a journey. It is sort of a North Star. You just keep living your life in a way that will help you get there in that direction and maybe get closer to it. Because I suspect fulfillment has a sense of 'that's it.' You're there. It's done. It's over. Where I do think we tend to be in perpetual motion. It's not bad having that North Star out there. You know, Walter Hagen said, 'you've got to smell the roses as you go by.' You can't be just phonetically involved. I think that's people like Eckhart Tolle and these guys write a lot about being in the moment. Which is actually truly enjoying. I must say, looking at this morning, I am looking out over the bay and it is absolutely gorgeous. I am thoroughly enjoying it. It would be easy not to. That's fulfillment.

The United States Olympic high-performance director Fin Kirwan:

I honestly do think there's a difference between satisfaction and fulfillment. Let me put it like this—I think I'll die satisfied but I'll never be fulfilled. I think that I'm satisfied with the work that I'm doing and I'm satisfied that I made the leap into sport and have been able to take advantage of the lucky breaks that I've got. And I'm satisfied that I'm doing the best job that I can and I'm really satisfied that I'm working with incredibly talented people. So I'm very, very satisfied. But I think fulfillment is something that you gotta keep going after. We have set internal goals here within the U.S. Olympic high performance team so see which are very, they are tough targets that we are setting for the games in Rio, tough targets in Tokyo in 2020, and so I think I'll always be looking at what's the next thing and how do I keep pushing on? And I think you'll find that with anybody that you're speaking with, that there are …once the next challenge has been achieved that they're already looking at where to go next and what's the next thing. And I find that that's a common theme in my life. I'm very satisfied with how I'm progressing and I'm working hard but I'll never entirely be fulfilled, you know…

The leadership speaker and executive coach Libby Gill:

First of all, I'm a parent, so fulfillment is two happy sons. They are so driven and purposeful themselves. I am so delighted when I see one of them is with a program that's actually global now, but it's called Teach for America. He is giving back by being a two-year teacher as part of his program in an inner-city school. My other son is a freshman in college at Oberlin and very politically active. To me, I couldn't ask for more. Fulfillment is that blend of meeting those personal passions and fulfilling those professional dreams. At this stage, as I'm approaching that other end of the work spectrum, I feel like I don't really have anything to prove, but I feel like I have a lot to give. That's a great place to be in life, so that's fulfillment.

What is that makes you fulfilled? Who close to you can you sit down with and talk it through? It's now one of my favorite coaching questions as it really gets my clients thinking about their answers.

The educational leader Dr. Phillip Matthews:

Fulfillment for me just implies you enjoy what you're doing. What you're doing therefore must be connected in some way to that passion. Yeah, you must enjoy the work that you're doing. You must find that there's an emotional connection. It's feeding an emotional need. It's connected emotionally to you, to what and who you are. I think fulfilled implies an end and I don't think driven people ever see an end. I think that they find it fulfilling, but I think it's a continuous journey and I don't think that they can stop. They never actually get there. I think when they get there it's kind of boring. The journey is more important than the destination. I can really identify with that in that the learning to play golf and then getting a par every hole is boring for me. It's the learning journey that for me is oh, that was great. I really hit that shot well. I find it quite boring hitting every shot well. I think there's no stimulation. There's no kind of emotion. There's no kind of frustration. It's boring. Same shot every time? No way.

The journey towards that point that is the most frustrating, stressful. Yeah and for me to use a golf analogy, if you get your handicap down to ten well, then you want be single figures. If you're single figures you want to be low single figures. If you're low single figures you want to be scratch. If you're scratch you want to be minus one. If you're minus one you want to turn pro. If you turn pro you want to win it. It never ends.

What does fulfillment look like to you the reader?

IS THIS THE END OR REALLY A NEW START TO A NEW YOU?

Thank you! That you have read this far means an awful lot to me.

It has given me great pleasure knowing that someone else might get inspired or motivated toward their dreams and goals. Everyone has drive, some just use it differently than others.

My drive to be a published author got me to this final place. Luckily I've enjoyed the journey along the way. It has had many challenges and at times I thought this would never work. Finding the time to write and put in energy and honesty is tough, but the vision pulled me along. The moment when you think of quitting but continue will always be the moment that brings you most satisfaction, and so it was. Halfway through writing this book, I felt well outside my comfort zone. I thought about putting the writing on the back burner. What if I am ridiculed? What if people don't like it? Luckily, I let my drive take over and pushed on to finish this book and all the work that goes with that. It's just my hard wired personality. I am a driven individual. My dreams will become reality, and my key dream is to inspire, help, and empower people all over the world to become the person they know they can be.

So, what's next?

The choice is yours. Are you going to live your life according to how others think you should live it or are you going to live your own life and do and dream what you want to become?

Taking small steps does indeed lead you to bigger success. Every journey really does begin with a small tiny step. It's the courage and tenacity to take that step that will define how far you can go. It might be something small now, but could lead to something big, something fulfilling.

Move forward. Shift gears.

Take that step. Dream big. Don't apologize to anyone for your dreams. They are yours and no one has a right to jump on them. Listen to people who will encourage you to achieve them, understand how you can help them achieve theirs. Lead with generosity and positivity.

Lead a fulfilled life. Don't live your life "measured out by coffee spoons." Live the life you dreamed of. Take time to understand what that means to you. Be bold and reach for your potential. Don't be typecast into your job or defined by what you have achieved to date.

Be happy now. Don't wait until tomorrow. Do something today that your future self will thank you for.

Bud Wilkinson once said, "Every game is an opportunity to measure yourself against your own potential. " Bud was the coach at the University of Oklahoma and apparently had an amazing impact on everyone.

If I were to choose one piece of advice that you take away from reading this book, it's just one word: DREAM.

Anything is possible if you dream it. If you want it bad enough and are eager to get there, then you'll get there. But first it's got to start with you dreaming.

I'll leave you with a blog post I wrote nearly a year ago now. Of all my blog posts this is the one that really helped me believe that I could write a book.

EVER HAD A DREAM?

One that repeats itself? Every now and again presses play when you least expect it. A dream that is a vivid picture of yourself doing something so defined and clear, that it feels real. A dream that feels so long and storied and complex, but in reality is only a few seconds in duration.

The emotions, the environment, sights, sounds, and smells seem so real, that you think about the dream well after you've woken up. It's an impactful dream. It's enough to propel you to take action, or enough to unsettle you. The average person has two to three dreams a night, believe it or not. What is the take away from those dreams for you? What clues do you get about yourself?

I have a dream like this.

I feel the warm sunlight on my face, as I stand arms by my side, facing out to sea. My eyes are closed. I hear the Pacific Ocean rolling in its waves with a repetitive chorus. The wind breezes softly, in that early evening way. Standing on a cliff path. I can hear people passing, but their chatter I don't hear. I open my eyes, then I turn to run. In the dream, I feel myself running along this cliff path, smiling, pushing myself a little. The ocean is to my left. The path has turns and twists, hills, pavement, and trail, and even an oceanside graveyard that I skip through. The corners, views, change in direction and even the little nuances of a sidewalk and how it can all ingrain itself in you, become part of you. It is etched now in my dream as it was when I ran it daily.

See, I've been here for real. It's a real run—one of my favorite runs of all time. Bondi Beach in Sydney has a cliff walk that goes for five kilometers to a neighboring beach, Coogee. When I lived there years ago, this was a run I used to do regularly (sometimes on my own, other times with my cousin Karen). It's a memory that has now morphed into this dream. My legs feel weightless (in reality I probably huffed and puffed my way through), and my arms in the dream are in perfect form (in reality, they hang at the sides sometimes when I run). However, in the dream I am weightless. I am happy. Life is full of potential. While my eyes dart to the path and back to the sea, I am in control. I go down to McKenzie's bay, then to Bronte and pass through Tamarama, (where Karen and her partner Brian had this amazing apartment with magnificent views) into

Clovelly and Gordon's Bay until all of sudden I'm at the end of the run on top of Coogee Beach, with its strong surf and deep sand. I turn around and run back.

I dream this every now and again, and it is incredibly powerful. This dream always occurs before or during a moment of change in my life. It must be my subconscious telling me about the journey ahead. After I have the dream, I feel strong. I have no fears, my confidence gets higher, and my sometime unbreakable resolve becomes superhero-like. I don't second-guess myself after it. I don't care what others will think, or if they pass comment when they read. I know that things will work out. The more weightless we are about our problems, the less they become problems.

> *"If you can dream it, you can achieve it."*
> **—Zig Ziglar**

As an Irish male, we don't tend to talk (or write) about dreams. It's a little too fluffy, I guess. I believe in them though and for me, usually it's a good day before or a good day after but it always keeps me focused on the future and the path ahead. It inspires me to live in the moment or reminds me that I am, well, just me. It gets me up earlier with a new zest for what I want to achieve.

One day, I will return to this particular part of the world. This will be the first run I'll do. My sister has now moved back to Sydney (in the last week), and we won't see each other for a while. We'll miss her around the place, but she has her own dreams to chase and create and I couldn't be happier for her. Maybe we can run it for real together someday.

There's always a group in the dream. One time, it was my children and wife laughing and having fun running behind me, or my sisters and their families, or all the relatives/friends walking the path. Other times, looking over the shoulder or passing a bench, it'd be someone that isn't here in real life anymore, but they're real in the dream playing a cameo role. My dad sitting there with his brother Joe. My grandparents on the next seat. They turn to say hello and smile and say, "Sit down for a minute and have a chat."

Powerful, good-for-the-soul dreaming.

So, happy dreaming, shift those gears and go achieve the life you want and realize your own high potential.

STAY IN TOUCH!

I'd like to invite you to connect with me and share your story of driving forward to your potential. Maybe together we can impact more lives and help those stuck in the grind of work, eating, TV, and little sleep. If you send them I promise to get back to you.

Tell me what your biggest dream was. What did you do to chase it? How did this book help you (or not).

Remember, my main goal here is to help people reach for their potential by using all the drives we discussed. That is why I want to hear your story. It might be oceans or continents between us but I want to make connections with driven people just like you and see how I can help them further.

Help me make the Shifting Gears concept internationally known. If you liked this read, connect, and let's start that dialogue or buy a copy for your business or your friends. Why not tweet a picture of you with the book, I'd be grateful? @ryanoreillyint is my twitter address.

www.ryanoreillyinternational.com has more podcast interviews with some very interesting people – sign up!

If you want me to speak to your group anywhere in the world, I will travel. This is now my passion, infusing others. I look forward to inspiring your team, conference, or seminar.

If you would like one-on-one coaching with me, then reach out and let me know. Coaching can propel you forward quicker than it might happen naturally. I am here to serve.

If you would like to attend one of my many scheduled events in the USA or Europe, please go to my website www.ryanoreillyinternational.com for details on the next event we plan to do in your area. If there isn't an event planned in your area, let me know and we'll get a crowd together in your local town or conference center. Let's spread this idea—potential—and let's help others shift their gears and reach their own high potential.

Email: ryan@highpotential.ie
Website: www.ryanoreillyinternational.com
Twitter: @ryanoreillyint
LinkedIn: Ryan O'Reilly High Potential International

An invitation from Ryan:
Be coached by Ryan by visiting www.ryanoreillyinternational.com
Book Ryan as a speaker at your next corporate event.

ACKNOWLEDGMENTS

When I sat down to write my first book, I wasn't sure where it was going to take me. I know using the term rollercoaster will seem like a cliché, but the process really was one of the hardest things I've completed. I am proud of the effort and it was a very cathartic experience. Of course like any big project or undertaking, you'll only get so far on your own, and the help, advice and support from key people helped me bring this project to a close and reach my dream of having a book published a reality.

It would be remiss of me not to mention and thank this fantastic and fun bunch of people. Without them not only would this project not have been completed, but it probably would not have even started. When you meet people who unselfishly help and want to help, you realize that others in your life are your cheerleaders. Sometimes we all need a little nudge in the right direction.

With that let me start the long list of thanks! First, I want to thank my wife, Annemarie, and my kids Michael, Emma and Liam for whom the book is dedicated. Every day I count my blessings and appreciate how lucky I am to have you all in my life. Fulfillment to me is seeing all of you balanced and happy and helping you reach your own goals in life. Happiness is the here and now—be that dinner or forest walks—and it's just being with you all that makes me happy. It is true now and always will be.

I want to thank my parents, Maureen and Michael who taught me plenty but more importantly loved me unconditionally, gave me the greatest gift of a fantastically happy childhood and who showed me that values and family above all else matter most. I'll never forget the heartbreaking passing of my father and how shattered my mother was. It was a love story with a sad end. He will always be with us in our dreams. My mother should know that spending time with her is still one of the greatest gifts and her greatest gift back is to just be content and happy.

I want to thank my three amazing sisters. Gillian, Cathy and Jean. Sometimes if you look closely you get motivated by those close to you and it's no different with my sisters. They are all inspiring mothers in their own right who are raising their children, who are honest, fair, kind and who have faced adversity and challenges head on. I am not sure I tell you enough but you're a great bunch and thank you for keeping me grounded and for your encouragement over the years. Happy memories are still being made with you and your families—long may that continue.

Thanks to my parents-in-law Mary and Tony and for all the support and advice you have offered over the years. I couldn't have asked for better parents-in-law and I look forward to the many happy times still ahead.

To my extended family of aunts, uncles, cousins, nieces, nephews, brothers-in-law, sisters-in-law, friends and best mate Aidan thank you for just being a solid fun bunch. I have learned and laughed plenty with you all over the years. I wish you continued happiness and am looking forward to those big family/friend reunions that will happen throughout life. Special thanks to those of you who encouraged my blog writing, something that started small as a hobby, which led me down this road of writing a book—thank you!

For those who took the time out of their busy schedules to be interviewed, many thanks for giving a relative stranger an interview and I'll be forever grateful you did. The interviews were all very motivating and inspired me to drive on.

In no particular order a big thank you to those interviews who feature Mark C. Thompson, Kingsley Aikins, Dr. Phillip Matthews, Mike Kafka, Jack Black, Stefan Trappitsch, Libby Gill, and Fin Kirwan.

For all those at the Morgan James Publishing house in New York, I'd like to acknowledge my appreciation for your faith in me and my book and also just your kind, friendly and professional approach to the whole process. I have enjoyed working with this bunch immensely and would highly recommend them to any author. Terry Whalin, Margo Toulouse, Nickcole Watkins, Jim Howard & David Hancock.

Many thanks are also due to my editor for the painstaking process of reading, correcting and offering guidance—a job I don't envy. Jamie Birdwell-Branson is a great editor and very professional. Best of luck for the future, Jamie—if there is a second book I know who to call! Thank you and wishing you and your family continued success.

No one man is an island and the idea of writing a book was a daunting prospect. For me it was a terrifying one as there was so much to do. *Where do I start? Will I be driven enough to complete it?* Luckily, I was able to connect with a writing coach. Julie Anne Eason (www.julieanneeason.com) was just magnificent, and kept me honest all the way through the process. Julie Anne is not just a writing coach, but more of an accountability one. She set targets for me and knew exactly how to get the best out of my writing, even when some weeks I'd leave our phone call more overwhelmed than ever. Pretty quickly into the process I realized that if it weren't for Julie then my drive to finish would not have been as persistent as it was. Julie, I'll be forever grateful for your patience, tenacity and great advice for helping me get my best writing out and getting this over the line. Notice I didn't include the words "super" "very" or "that" that much and I now laugh every time I hear myself saying any of the three! Wishing you and your family continued success in your pursuits and in life.

Finally, thanks to you, the reader and may your DRIVE carry you on to fulfill your dreams. Arthur Lydiate summed it up best when he said, "there is an Olympian in every village." The challenge is what are you going to do now to show that you can be that "Olympian" or help someone else realize their potential, help them become the "Olympian" in their chosen field. Best of luck and I look forward to hearing how you go!

ABOUT THE AUTHOR

 As a professional speaker and executive coach, Ryan helps business leaders and entrepreneurs build high performing teams, break through plateaus and realize their true potential. Ryan worked for fifteen years as a senior sales leader for three Fortune 100 Tech Companies, including Apple and Dell, and has worked in California, Australia, the UK, and Ireland. At time of writing, Ryan is studying for his Masters Degree (MSc.) in Personal & Business Coaching at University College Cork, Ireland. Ryan is also an Associate Certified Coach (ACC) with the International Coaching Federation (ICF) and in 2015 was nominated as a finalist in the *ICF Ireland* Coach of the Year awards.

Taking that experience with him, Ryan now follows his true passion, which is helping others drive forward and reach their dreams. Ryan is also an adventure cyclist and keen marathoner and uses the lessons he learns from sports in his keynote speeches, workshops and 1:1 coaching sessions. Ryan travels worldwide for his clients.

Having previously lived, studied, and worked in the USA, the UK, and Australia, Ryan now lives with his wife and three children in Cork, Ireland.

Printed in the USA
CPSIA information can be obtained
at www.ICGtesting.com
JSHW082340140824
68134JS00020B/1794

9 781630 478520